# THE

# NITRATE

# BOATS

Cover: ANGLO-CHILEAN being swung by the tug DONGARA in London Docks. Portrayed by artist's licence, this never happened as ANGLO-CHILEAN was sold two years before the tug was completed. The United Steam Tug Co Ltd, Gravesend (''Ring Tugs'') held the Anglo Line towage contract. Note the tug's British India funnel colours, United Steam Tug having been formed by Gravesend pilots in 1890 to handle B.I. ships. They were absorbed by William Watkins & Co in 1937.(Painting by Laurence Dunn)

"Unconquerable". Captain Parslow on the bridge of ANGLO-CALIFORNIAN, 4 July 1915, with his son at the wheel and U39 attacking. The original was painted by Thomas M. Hemy (1852-1937) to record the posthumous Victoria Cross awarded to Captain Parslow for the defence of his ship. The painting hung in Sir John Latta's office. As the present whereabouts, or existence, of the original is unknown this was re-painted from a small black and white print published in "The Shipping World", 1920.                                    (Painting by Keith Byass)

# The
# NITRATE BOATS

**David Burrell**

By the same author:
    Scrap & Build
    The Thistle Boats
    The Den Line
    Furness Withy 1891-1991

Published by the World Ship Society, 28 Natland Road, Kendal LA9 7LT, England

Printed by William Gibbons & Sons Ltd., Wolverhampton, England

ISBN 0.905617.77.0

# CONTENTS

# ACKNOWLEDGEMENTS

In the heyday of British shipping there were many semi-liner companies about whom little has been written despite the interesting matters with which they were associated. One such was the Nitrate Producers' Steamship Company Ltd formed in 1895. Sadly, being wound up under wartime conditions in 1942, nothing has survived of their office records.

Having become interested in the company some twenty years ago the story has slowly come together despite difficulties in tracing material information on some aspects, such as finding the Lawther family, the record of WINKFIELD's Manchester Ship Canal accident and unravelling the Yukon gold story. As information developed the story became more interesting.

The bibliography includes some of the works I have consulted over the years, also newspapers and magazines which have proved of value in supplying anything from clues to full data. The following is an incomplete list of organisations and people whose willing help I appreciate and acknowledge. Over such a time span there are certain to be others I have missed, if you are such the fault is mine and not intentional, and I tender my apologies.

Belfast Public Library, Belfast; Bibliothek für Zeitgeschichte, Stuttgart; Dawson City Museum & Historical Society, Yukon; Department of Transport Marine Library, London; Germanischer Lloyd, Hamburg; Guildhall Library, London; Lloyd's Register of Shipping, London; Manchester Ship Canal Co Ltd, Manchester; Ministry of Defence, London (Naval & Air Historical Branches); National Maritime Museum, Greenwich; Public Record Office, London; Spink & Son Ltd, London; Sunderland Museum & Art Gallery, Sunderland; Tyne & Wear Archives, Newcastle.

Dr L. Appal-Olsen; D. Ashby; D. Briggs; G. Brooke; J.K. Byass; R. Campbell; N. Castelli (Trieste); P. Dalton; Mrs M. Dobie (née Latta); L. Dunn; I.J. Farquhar (Dunedin); A. Greenway; R. Haggar (Vancouver); L. Harrison; N. Hechler (Seevetal); H. Hignett; S.C. Heal (Vancouver); D.R. Hudson; J. Hunter; E.L. Johnson (Vancouver); W.I. Latta: B.W. Lawley; S. Lord; A. McArdle; Mrs M.A. Mair (née Latta); P. Marshall; E. Menzies; D. Milburn; E.E. Milburn; J.C. Moffat; A.J. Moore; E.A. Munday; A.G. Osler; G. Rea; R. Robinson; I.W. Rooke; R.J. Scarlett; W.A. Schell (Holbrook, Mass.); J.H. Short; R.C. Sinclair; C.R. Snape; E.N. Taylor; A.J. Tennent; J. Winser.

Illustrations are acknowledged with sources where known, but from experience I know how difficult it is to be certain these are correct. I tender my apologies for any errors which may have crept in.

I am certain some readers will be in a position to amplify, add to or correct text. I welcome any further information to enable my master text to be corrected.

Finally, and not least, my thanks to my wife for her forebearance as this file has grown and spread in our house.

Cumnock,                                                                          November, 1995
Ayrshire KA18 3BJ.

# INTRODUCTION

"The Nitrate Producers' Steamship Company Ltd, sometimes called the Anglo Line, were the most favourite of liner tramps to visit the West Coast between the years of 1900 and the 1930s. These "Anglo" vessels, specially built for this run, were looked upon as the aristocrats on the Coast. It was a pleasure to one and all when they came in and this they did without any fuss at all. The masters knew their business from A to Z, were persona grata everywhere and much respected by everyone with whom they came in contact. Who does not remember such names as Parsons, Parslow, Isaacs, Westacott, Lewis, etc?"

So wrote a West Coaster in Sea Breezes (March 1947) after many years working in Chile. Little has been written about the shipping enterprise founded by John Latta and managed by Lawther, Latta and Company and it is hoped this account will help fill that gap.

*ANGLO-SAXON (2) at Adelaide.*                    *(I.J. Farquhar Collection)*

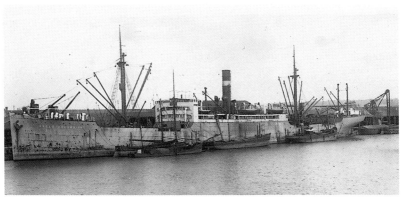

*Two views of a weather-worn ANGLO-COLOMBIAN, the only second-hand ship purchased for the Anglo Line*

# LATTA AND LAWTHER                  *1*

Driving down a quiet country lane in Ayrshire a farm name drew my attention, Darmalloch sounded familiar. A moment's thought to recall this was the childhood home of a vigorous and controversial London shipping entrepreneur and believer in free trade, John Latta. Described by some who met him as a slim, dapper, youngish figure (in spite of advancing years) with sparkling pince-nez, while others recalled him as a rather grim and forbidding figure, he established and built one of the most successful tramp shipping fleets to fly the red ensign. As befitted his Victorian upbringing he held strong views on the management of business, views he was not afraid to voice in his frank and definite manner. Although not active to any degree in the Chamber of Shipping, or other trade and public organisations, these views were always noted and given serious consideration. Neither was he beholden to the views and attitudes of the majority if he considered them wrong, as was evident when he offered Captain Stanley Lord of the CALIFORNIAN command of his best ships after the unwarranted censure of Lord following the tragic loss of the TITANIC.

Born on 9 May 1867 John Latta was the son of William Latta, JP. His grandfather had moved from Ayr to Cumnock and was the carrier from Cumnock to Edinburgh in those pre-railway days, a long and difficult drive on unsurfaced roads. He frequently carried out missions for the Marquess of Bute when in Edinburgh, duties that led to considerable trust and the offer of the farm. The census of 1851 confirms 30 year old bachelor William Latta in residence, with his elder sister Isabella as housekeeper. In the previous 1841 census Latta is not listed at Darmalloch, hence the tenancy was taken in the intervening years. On 26 October 1858 William married Margaret Allan and, in the years that followed, the 300 acre farm was to be home to a growing family of five boys and four girls. John, the second son and fourth child was, in later years, to be joined in his shipping business by his younger brothers William (born 1861) and Andrew (1874).

Although Darmalloch is not now held by the family, until recently they farmed at Glenmuirshaw and Kyle further up the Glenmuir Water to the east of Cumnock, and their town house at the top of the Barrhill, Cumnock, still stands as one of the first houses seen by travellers approaching the town along the A70 road from Edinburgh and Muirkirk.

John Latta completed his education at Ayr Academy and having from an early age chosen a career in shipping was sent to Greenock to learn his trade in the office of Craig, Scott and Company, owners and managers of a fleet of sailing ships. It is not known what William Latta's training was, but Andrew Latta was apprenticed as a bank clerk.

The Square, Old Cumnock

*Cumnock about 1900, as it was known by John Latta.
(Cumnock Library)*

*Glaisnock Street, Cumnock*

With the confidence engendered by this training John Latta, on attaining his majority at the age of 21, moved to London and took a position as chartering clerk with Trinder, Anderson and Company, and then with Little and Johnston. This further experience completed, in 1892 he joined with Robert Lawther to enter business as Lawther, Latta and Company.

| Fleet of Craig, Scott and Company, Greenock | | | | |
|---|---|---|---|---|
| Name | Blt/Acq | GT | Type* | Disposal* |
| LADY GERTRUDE | 67/80 | 524 | w.bk | 1887 sold. |
| ex Pace | | | | |
| KAHLAMBA | 56/84 | 1856 | i.bk | 1887 sold. |
| ex Carlos | | | | |
| GEORGE GILROY | 62/84 | 1862 | w.bk , | 1888 condemned. |
| SUPREME | 76/85 | 764 | w.bk | 1887 sold. |
| Ardgowan S.N. Co Ltd | | | | |
| ARDGOWAN | 83 | 296 | i.ss | 1885 sold. |
| Seaforth Ship Co Ltd | | | | |
| SEAFORTH | 62/83 | 1189 | i.bk | 1894 sold. |
| Howden Iron Sailing Ship Co Ltd | | | | |
| HOWDEN | 55/86 | 1205 | i.bk | 1896 sold. |

A year older than his partner, Robert Lawther was an Ulsterman, born in Londonderry on the 26th May 1866, the son of Samuel Lawther, a leading Belfast shipowner. Francis Cunynghame, who knew him well, described him in the following words —

"Lawther was a very likeable Irishman, a great big fellow, had plenty of money and lived well." Born in 1833 Samuel Lawther was the son of Robert Lawther of Islandreagh, near Antrim. As a youth Samuel moved to Belfast to work in a shipping office. Soon he launched into business on his own account, in 1858 being appointed agent for three of Canada's largest timber exporters. Over the years a prosperous business developed in the partnership of Lawther and Harvey. To carry their trade a large fleet of North American built sailing ships was managed. In addition an interest was developed in the coal trade under the banner of the Mersey Coal Company. As a public figure in Belfast for forty years he was a councillor (1872-1882) and Alderman (1882-1910) of the Corporation, High Sheriff of the County of the City of Belfast (1902) and

| Name | Blt/Acq | GT | Type* | Disposal* |
|---|---|---|---|---|
| **Fleet of Samuel Lawther and Sons, Belfast** | | | | |
| ANN AUGUSTA | 56/66 | 645 | w.bk | 29.1.1868 ashore, sold, bu. |
| CYPRUS | 61/67 | 214 | w.bgn | 4.12.1869 wrecked. |
| PAWNEE | 68/69 | 672 | w.bk | 3.1.1871 ashore, condemned, bu |
| FALKLAND | 56/70 | 968 | w.sh | 1.1871 wrecked. |
| LOTHAIR | 63/70 | 649 | w.bk | 1891 sold. |
| ex Agnes M Lovitt | | | | |
| FOREST QUEEN | 62/71 | 549 | w.bk | 1887 sold. |
| ELLEN | 63/73 | 857 | w.bk | 1878 bu. |
| ex Mercur | | | | |
| HOWARD | 64/73 | 613 | w.bk | 1878 sold. |
| MARIA | 63/73 | 603 | w.bk | 9.1.1877 abandoned. |
| L G BIGLOW | 66/74 | 583 | w.bk | 1885 sold. |
| PROTECTOR (tug) | 69/74 | 89 | w.ps | 1886 sold. |
| E J HARLAND | 75 | 1333 | i.sh | 19.11.1879 collision. |
| EVA | 58/75 | 412 | w.bk | 1881 bu. |
| FANNY ATKINSON | 65/75 | 626 | w.bk | 7.2.1887 foundered. |
| PRESTO | 63/75 | 642 | w.bk | 8.7.1878 abandoned. |
| SAVANNA | 68/75 | 771 | w.bk | 8.2.1886 ashore, sold. |
| G W WOLFF | 78 | 1743 | i.sh | 1902 sold. |
| WALTER H WILSON | 82 | 2518 | i.4bk | 1900 sold. |
| W J PIRRIE | 83 | 2576 | i.4bk | 1898 sold. |
| QUEEN'S ISLAND | 85 | 2093 | i.bk | 1890 sold. |
| CUBA | 83/91 | 2047 | i.ss | 1892 sold. |
| A J BALFOUR | 92 | 3467 | s.ss | 1896 sold. |
| NOEL | 75/92 | 851 | w.bk | 22.12.1894 wrecked. |
| ROMANOFF | 76/92 | 1086 | w.bk | 1895 sold. |
| RUTH PALMER | 74/92 | 965 | w.bk | 25.4.1894 sunk in ice. |
| 1891 Belfast & Mersey S.S. Co Ltd | | | | |
| 1929 Belfast, Mersey & Manchester S.S. Co Ltd (to 1944) | | | | |
| MANCHESTER | 91 | 506 | s.ss | 1933 bu. |
| FLESWICK | 00/29 | 610 | s.ss | 1936 bu. |
| STORMONT | 99/29 | 1031 | s.ss | 20.11.1946 collision. |
| ex Saltees | | | | |
| GREYPOINT | 05/33 | 1123 | s.ss | 1950 bu. |
| ex Rathlin | | | | |
| MOUNTSTEWART | 07/36 | 1099 | s.ss | 1950 bu. |
| ex Pladda | | | | |

*Abbreviations: w = wood, i = iron, s = steel, bgn = brigantine, bk = barque, 4bk = 4-masted barque, sh = ship, ps = paddle steamer, ss = screw steamship, bu = broken up.

*Sir John Latta.*

a Harbour Commissioner (1882-1909). In 1869 he was one of the original shareholders in the Oceanic Steam Navigation Company Ltd, better known as the White Star Line.

In 1876, in partnership with Thomas Dixon, Samuel Lawther ordered the iron full rigger E.J. HARLAND from Harland and Wolff. The toss of a coin gave management to Lawther. Dixon responded by taking an order left on the hands of Harland and Wolff, placing her in service as LORD CAIRNS (iron ship, built 1877/1373gt). Over the next decade the two responded to each other's orders, Lawther's G.W. WOLFF matching Dixon's LORD DUFFERIN (iron ship 79/1778gt), WALTER H. WILSON with LORD DOWNSHIRE (iron 4-masted barque 82/2322gt) and W.J. PIRRIE was a sister of LORD WOLSELEY (iron 4-masted ship 83/2577gt). Finally Lawther's QUEEN'S ISLAND, the largest 3-masted barque ever built, matched LORD TEMPLETON (iron ship 86/2152gt). Also in 1876 Samuel Lawther had, in agreement with the Pennsylvania Railroad, placed his ships on the berth from Philadelphia to Belfast and Dublin, G.W. WOLFF being specifically intended for this Delaware trade.

Samuel's two sons, Robert Allen and Henry Stanley, joined him in these business interests, the timber and shipping agents Lawther and Harvey, and S. Lawther and Sons who both managed ships in world trade and the Belfast and Mersey Steamship Company Ltd, formed in 1891 jointly with J.J. Mack and Sons Ltd, Liverpool, to ply between Belfast and the Mersey. They also acted as Belfast agents for the Belfast and Manchester Steamship Company, an unincorporated body that worked alongside the Belfast and Mersey

*MANCHESTER*                                   *(A. Greenway Collection)*

12

*Robert Lawther*

Steamship Company Ltd. For some years Samuel Lawther had been a director of the Belfast Steamship Company Ltd and, in 1889, when the chairmanship became vacant expected to be elected. This did not transpire; Lawther never attended another meeting and the formation of the Belfast and Mersey Steamship Company followed, to compete with the older company for many years between Belfast Lough and the Mersey.

With the Manchester Ship Canal under construction, it was planned the company steamer would, after calling at Liverpool, proceed up to Manchester. The canal opened in 1894 and thereafter a twice weekly service was advertised between Belfast and Manchester. The only vessel owned, MANCHESTER (built 1891, 506gt), remained in service until broken up in 1933. An option with the builders for a second ship was not taken up, instead ships owned by J.J. Mack and Sons were employed. The company was superseded by a new company formed in 1929, the Belfast, Mersey and Manchester Steamship Company Ltd, the year a second ship, FLESWICK,

### Sir Henry Morton Stanley, GCB (1841-1904)

Samuel Lawther named his second son, born in 1871, Henry Stanley Lawther for the famous explorer and journalist who, as a friend, stayed with the family when visiting Belfast. Like Colonel North, Stanley wove a web of fiction into his life which makes evaluation difficult.

Born illegitimate at Denbigh, Wales, his mother, Betsy Parry, named him John Rowlands. He landed at New Orleans in 1859 and adopted the name Henry Stanley, from a merchant he portrayed as his benefactor. Joining the Confederate army he was captured at Shiloh, the first major battle of the American Civil War, and later served in the Union army and navy.

Turning to journalism he achieved fame as special correspondent of the New York Herald, accompanying the Abyssinian expedition (1868). He attended the opening of the Suez Canal (1869) before undertaking an expedition to meet David Livingstone at Ujiji (Lake Tanganyika), 10 November 1871. Further exploration followed, the Ashanti Expedition (1873), completion of Livingstone's work (1874-7), founding the Congo Free State for King Leopold II of Belgium (culminating in the 1884-5 Congress of Berlin) and the relief of Emin Pasha, the sole surviving and isolated Sudanese district governor after Khartoum fell to the Mahdi in 1885 (1887-9).

He married (1890), renounced the American citizenship taken in 1885 to re-naturalise as British (1892) and was elected Liberal-Unionist MP for North Lambeth (1895-1900). A knighthood followed in the 1899 Birthday Honours, Knight Grand Cross of the Most Honourable Order of the Bath. Ill health, partly attributed to his time in Africa, led to his death in May 1904.

was added. Ultimately, in April 1945, this undertaking became part of the Coast Lines Group as a subsidiary of the Belfast Steamship Company Ltd. In addition to the coastal liner trade of the Belfast and Mersey Company, a brief foray was made into deep-sea steam with the second-hand CUBA and newly built A.J. BALFOUR, named for the chief secretary for Ireland and, later, prime minister.

Robert served a five year apprenticeship with Harland and Wolff, then made a two year trip round the world. Sailing from Liverpool as a guest of White Star on the CELTIC in late October 1887 he reached San Francisco a month later and found W.J. PIRRIE and QUEEN'S ISLAND there. He arranged charters, sending the PIRRIE in ballast to Manila for a cargo of sugar and QUEEN'S ISLAND to Newcastle, NSW, to load coal for San Francisco. He chose to sail with QUEEN'S ISLAND on 28 February 1888 on what was to be a 44 day passage to Australia.

Following his return to Belfast Robert Lawther spent a period superintending the Lawther fleet before joining a London shipping office, and then linking with John Latta in their new venture in 1892. Henry also served his time with Harland and Wolff before entering his father's office where he remained when

---

### Farewell to a Nitrate Port
by "Eildon"*

*There's a port to which I've been, it's the smallest ever seen,*
*To call it port is really quite a sin;*
*It lies snugly tucked away in a corner of a bay,*
*And known on Chile's shores as sweet Junin.*

*Should your cargo be of coals they will take it out in doles,*
*Some new, some old and secondhand and thin,*
*But just to cause delay each sling you'll have to weigh,*
*For 'tis the custom of the port of sweet Junin.*

*But should you load with nitre they will send it in a lighter —*
*By pulling hard the ship's side it may win,*
*For of lighters they've got plenty—they've got eighteen, nineteen, twenty*
*To do the work of fifty in Junin.*

*Most Chile ports are small, but this is tiniest of them all,*
*Its streets create no bustle or no din,*
*Yet you can proudly brag of a British Consul's flag*
*That floats o'er Garratts' office in Junin.*

*Then again you have no zoo or museum, it is true;*
*Some ports have these, though they're not worth a pin,*
*But of the fleas upon the coast you can safely boast,*
*Which congregate in millions in Junin.*

*Good luck and happy lives to my friends there and their wives,*
*I toast their health in ginger and in gin,*
*For though their port be small they've the largest hearts of all —*
*I'll ne'er forget their kindness in Junin.*

---

*Quoted from Sea Breezes, January 1947. The identity of "Eildon" is not known, other than he was master of one of Raeburn and Verel's steamers.

Robert moved to London, being appointed Managing Director of the Belfast and Mersey Steamship Company Ltd. In due course Lawther and Harvey were appointed agents for the Anglo-American Oil Company Ltd, later renamed the Esso Petroleum Company Ltd, a subsidiary of the Standard Oil Company (New Jersey).

Initially the common background shared by the two partners in Lawther, Latta and Company saw them concentrating on deep sea chartering of sailing ships, seeking cargo for the Clyde and Belfast fleets with which they were familiar. One of the trades actively pursued was the shipment of nitrates from the West Coast of South America to European and other destinations. In those days prior to the development of an industrial process to produce nitrogen, demand for Chilean nitrate was growing, especially in the German and French sugar-beet fields.

The main problem in the trade centred on delays due to the primitive facilities at Pisagua and other Chilean ports. Ships took months to load two or three thousand tons bag by bag from lighters at open anchorages, risky berths subject to inclement weather coming in off the Pacific, such as the hurricane which hit Iquique, Junin and Pisagua on 22 June 1911. During the afternoon the sea had a dirty appearance and an unusually long and heavy swell. A thick camanchaca (hill winter mist) hung very low over the coast and totally obliterated the hills. That evening, commencing between 7 pm and 8 pm, one of the worst gales known on the coast raged for three hours, enormous seas accompanied by hurricane force winds from the north, sandstorms, earth tremors and rain, and chaos in the anchorage. Some 200 deaths were reported. Many vessels and lighters were damaged and lost, at Iquique the Italian CAVALIERE CIAMPA foundered and the French MADELEINE was beached and became a total loss, whilst at Caleta Buena the German ADELAIDE was lost. Lawther Latta's SOUTH AUSTRALIA was at Junin and suffered damage in collision with the ALEXANDRIA. Others were driven out to sea, like the barque ROWENA which took several days to reach port again in tow of Andrew Weir's WYMERIC.

*Iquique harbour about 1893-1895.*      *(National Maritime Museum)*

# THE NITRATE KING 2

Soon after commencing business John Latta visited the West Coast under an arrangement with "Colonel" J.T. North—the "Nitrate King"—with a view to arranging for Lawther, Latta and Company to represent North and Jewell, Iquique, as London chartering agents. John North, a controversial entrepreneur, is the third person to feature in the origin of the Nitrate Producers' Steamship Company Ltd.

It is at times difficult to differentiate between fact and the fairytale account of his life that North was wont to encourage—in more recent times it would likely be said he was "economical with the truth". For example, the writer of his obituary appreciation in "The Times" (6 May 1896) was led to write
"when the conquering Chilians came to seize upon the lands they found the British flag flying over many square miles of nitrate beds".

John Thomas North was born near Leeds on 30 January 1842 and trained as an engineer with the Hunslet firm of Shaw, North and Watson. Completing his apprenticeship he moved to Fowler and Company, Leeds, in 1865, married Jane Woodhead and two years later was sent by them to Chile to supervise locomotive erection for the Carrizal Railway. Leaving their employ in 1871 he stayed in South America, moving to Iquique, Peru, where he gained experience of the nitrate business working on the oficina owned by Gonzalez Veliz before going into partnership as North and Jewell, machinery importers and steamship agents. Maurice Jewell was also Lloyd's Agent and the first British Vice-Consul. At the same time North became involved in water supply, a key matter in the Atacama Desert, and this led to a supply monopoly being established.

Meanwhile Peru had reached a state of penury which the Government tried to retrieve in 1875 by expropriating the nitrate producing plants, or oficinas, paying the owners in bonds. These bonds rapidly depreciated and were subject to speculation when The War of the Pacific broke out in 1879 between Chile and Bolivia/Peru. In 1879 bonds were selling at 60% of their face value, later falling to 10-15%. Chile rapidly proved the victor, in 1880 occupying the Bolivian province of Atacama and the Peruvian province of Tarapaca. Lima fell to Chilean forces in 1881. By the Treaty of Ancon in October 1883 Peru also ceded the provinces of Arica and Tacna, although Tacna was returned to Peru in 1929.

In 1881 Chile decided to return the oficinas in the conquered territory to the holders of the bonds, many of which had found their way into the hands of North and his partner, John Harvey. The following year North returned to England to settle his family and commence his career as a company promoter.

*John Thomas North.*

Backed by the Liverpool merchant house of W. and J. Lockett, North now incorporated his first nitrate company on 3 February 1883, the year in which Locketts launched the iron barque J.T. NORTH. The relationship between North and Lockett was further strengthened when, in 1892, his daughter Emma North married George Alexander Lockett. The Liverpool Nitrate Company Ltd was capitalised at £150,000 and purchased the Oficina Ramirez for £50,000. North had earlier acquired the bonds, which had a nominal value of £13,750, for £5,000. This inflation of securities, plus highly inflated capital, repeated in the many companies that followed, brought wealth to North and condemnation from some financial observers and writers who recognised the method and warned investors. However, in the main, the salesmanship of North prevailed.

Within the next decade North truly became "The Nitrate King" with Tarapaca his fiefdom. Control of numerous nitrate companies (including the Colorado, Lagunas, Liverpool, Paccha & Jazpampa and Primativa Nitrate Companies), the water supply (Tarapaca Waterworks Company Ltd), railway (Nitrate Railways Company Ltd), a bank (Bank of Tarapaca and London Ltd), import and supplies (Nitrate Provisions Supply Company Ltd) and other businesses saw him in a position to influence what he did not own. He manipulated his portfolio of companies to maintain investors' confidence, although when any company collapsed he usually had few shares left in his name. Elsewhere in Chile he invested heavily in the coal mines of the southern province of Arauco, through the mine and railway owning Arauco Company Ltd. His interests were not limited to Chile, they included tin mines at Maravillas in Bolivia, quicksilver at Ripanji some 15 miles from Belgrade (Ripanji Quicksilver and Silver Mining Company Ltd) and gold in South Africa (the Spes Bona mine), as well as North's Navigation Collieries (1889) Ltd producing Welsh coal from mines in Glamorgan.

In 1887 North had purchased the important Lagunas nitrate field for £110,000, although it was to be some time before this was developed. Before he died in 1896 three oficinas had been erected at Lagunas, the railway extended to serve them and the Lagunas Nitrate Company Ltd floated in 1894 to buy one of the oficinas for £850,000.

As might be expected North became a controversial figure in Chile where political crisis was to develop to the Revolution of 1891. Jose Balmaceda had become President in 1886, and from then to his suicide at the end of the Revolution the crisis between the legislature and executive deepened. The nitrate capitalists proved a convenient bogey, a large percentage of Government income coming from a tax on nitrate exports. When producers combined, limiting production to maintain price levels in a saturated market, it brought accusations of anti-Government action as this reduced the amount of duty collected. This brings to mind similar situations which have since arisen, under parallel circumstances, in some oil producing countries. Strangely, in Chile after the Revolution, the hostility to British nitrate interests became more bitter than in the Balmaceda period and a myth developed portraying Balmaceda as the martyr for truth, nobility and justice, and North the personification of perfidy, ambition and greed. Neither was valid.

Made the first Freeman of the City of Leeds in 1889, North collapsed and died in his office during a meeting of directors of the Buenaventura Nitrate Company Ltd on 5 May 1896. His sudden departure from the scene proved detrimental to many of his companies, whose fortunes suffered from the absence of his optimism, which had kept them alive and thriving on the Stock Exchange.

# NITRATE PRODUCERS'         *3*

North spoke of forming a shipping company during his last visit to Chile in 1889, but took no action to pursue this logical development of his interests. During his visit in 1892 Latta found a ready response to the suggestion that steam should be introduced into the nitrate trade, but initially North was reluctant to give it his backing.

Writing during 1935, in the 2001st issue of the magazine "Syren and Shipping", John Latta referred to the occasion when this reluctance was overcome. Visiting Colonel North in his office on business Latta concluded by congratulating him as his horse Nunthorpe had just won (22 July 1892) the Liverpool Cup, ridden by "Morny" Cannon, also on his greyhound Fullarton winning the Waterloo Cup in four successive years (1889-1892). Latta then sallied that North's racing colours (light blue, primrose sleeves, primrose 5-pointed stars and scarlet cap) would look well on the funnel of a steamer which could, carrying nitrate cargo controlled by North, prove a profitable venture. North was sold on the idea and called in several of his nitrate associates, immediately assigning them shares in the new company. Latta returned to his office with promises to take up £39,000 of the capital of a yet to be formed company already in his pocket.

As the above conversation would appear to have taken place in the late summer or early autumn of 1892, and the first steamer was not laid down until July 1894, there seems to have been a delay of some eighteen months in implementation.

The order was placed with Short Brothers, the Sunderland shipbuilders, and launched on 24 January 1895 as COLONEL J.T. NORTH. The title Colonel, North being Honorary Colonel of the 2nd Tower Hamlets Engineers Volunteers, was necessary as Locketts in Liverpool still had the J.T. NORTH.

*Built for W. & J. Lockett in 1883 and sold in 1898, the J.T. NORTH later became the Danish JOHAN and was sunk by U79 on 26 December 1916. John Masefield wrote "... the perfect J.T. NORTH, the loveliest barque my city has sent forth."*
*(National Maritime Museum)*

Soon after the launch, on 4 March 1895, The Nitrate Producers' Steamship Company Ltd was incorporated to own the steamer, with a capital of £100,000 in 20,000 £5 shares. This was to be increased in December 1907 to £400,000 (half as £5 5% cumulative preference shares, and half £5 ordinary shares) to accommodate the purchase and integration of the assets of the Southern Steam Shipping Company Ltd and Seafield Shipping Company Ltd by means of an exchange of shares.

The association with Short Brothers was to last, no newbuilding order was ever to be placed with another yard. In a more personal vein John Latta also found a bride on Wearside, leading Ada May Short, John Short's daughter, to the altar there on 17 March 1896 to cement the close alliance that was to continue in family and business. I have also heard North was related to the Short family by marriage, although I have yet to identify the link. Lawther, Latta and Company became the London insurance brokers for all Short Brothers' business and the quotation books of the shipyard contain numerous instances of offers to build being made to prospective owners through John Latta's agency. Regrettably, apart from a submission to John Heron and Company, Liverpool, in October 1902 (which was never built), the quotation books do not name the clients concerned. Lawther, Latta and Company also undertook coal sales, ballasting ships outwards to the West Coast with coal and selling parcels on arrival through the agency of George Kenrick, a retired Australian jockey and very successful shipping agent on the coast. Their Chilean contacts led to other business, such as in December 1901 when they purchased IDAHO (built 1898, 6308gt) from Thomas Wilson, Sons and Company, Hull, for £80,000 on behalf of the Chilean Government who employed her as RANCAGUA until disposing of her by scuttling in March 1931.

By the end of 1896 three ships were at sea with the yellow star on blue over red banded funnel of Nitrate Producers'. COLONEL J.T. NORTH had been followed by AVERY HILL, launched on 6 June 1895 by Mrs North, and JUANITA NORTH, launched on 13 May 1896. AVERY HILL was named for North's home at Eltham, Kent, and JUANITA NORTH for his wife Jane. Although not sisters all were similar spar deckers, Latta having adopted this design, which was later to develop into the shelter decker, for the sheltered cubic capacity available when high bulk cargo was carried. All were powered by triple expansion engines giving a speed of ten knots. William Allan and Company supplied that for COLONEL J.T. NORTH and George Clark Ltd the machinery for the other two.

COLONEL J. T. NORTH was taken to sea by John Petersen, a Norwegian master with a British ticket, who remained with the company until the ship was sold and then took service with other owners. He was joined in January 1896 by Charles Hullah who, after a year as mate, transferred to take AVERY HILL when James Parsons took GEORGE FLEMING. Herbert Perry was mate of the COLONEL J. T. NORTH before Hullah. Born in Herefordshire in 1847 Perry had had his certificate suspended following the loss of his command, the Pacific Steam Navigation Company's JOHN ELDER wrecked North of Talcahuano in January 1892. With Latta he was again promoted to command JUANITA NORTH in July 1896, followed by various of the fleet until signing off ANGLO-SAXON in November 1906 to retire.

James Parsons had joined the new company as master of AVERY HILL. A Somerset man whose first command was the London registered steamer JENNY OTTO in 1887, he left her to take Latta's new ship in August 1895 and remained in command with his new employers until retiring from the sea at the age of 62, signing off ANGLO-BOLIVIAN on 24 October 1913.

In 1895 the two new steamers took their first cargoes, coal to Genoa (AVERY HILL) and Savona (COLONEL J.T. NORTH) and then on to the Black Sea to load grain for Antwerp and Rotterdam respectively. In October and November they both undertook their first visits to Chile, COLONEL J.T. NORTH arriving at Pisagua on 9 December and AVERY HILL soon after at Valparaiso and Iquique. Both were short voyage designs built for Atlantic and Black Sea trades and proved unsuitable to the long distance nitrate routes. The major problem, however, was dispatch, as the sailing ships were loaded in small parcels over an extended period of time. These new steamers not only took a cargo twice the size of that carried by sail (COLONEL J.T. NORTH could take 4,200 tons), they also required to load much faster and the facilities were not there to handle this dispatch. So after these experimental loadings the company ships were not to return to the West Coast for several years. The situation changed rapidly and in 1900 North could report at the Annual General Meeting no difficulty in loading much larger 7,000 ton steamers at a rate of 1,500 tons a day, compared with the 50 to 100 tons a day a few years earlier.

Captain Perry took JUANITA NORTH when new, transferring to ANGLO-CHILIAN when she entered service. Robert Calvert joined the company in June 1898 to take over JUANITA NORTH, and remained with the company for the rest of his seagoing career which ended when he came ashore from ANGLO-MEXICAN in July 1913.

Until the end of 1897 the three ships were largely confined to Atlantic and Mediterranean tramp trades, COLONEL J.T. NORTH was also chartered for three months in December 1896 for trade between Buenos Aires and Rio de Janeiro. She was the first ship to leave the fleet. Having taken coal to Port Said she arrived at Liverpool on 12 October 1897 with grain from Sulina and was sold to Austrian interests and renamed ISTOK. As such she was seized by Russian forces at Taganrog on the outbreak of World War I and on 24 December 1914 was one of four ships used in an attempt to close the Turkish coal port of Zonguldak with mines and blockships. The other three were OLEG (59/1125gt), ATHOS (91/1742gt) and ERNA (99/1539gt). The Russian force came into contact with Turkish and German units, including BRESLAU which damaged OLEG. ATHOS was scuttled after being shelled and the remaining two blockships scuttled uselessly in deep water off Zonguldak under fire from coastal batteries.

AVERY HILL also had a relatively short life with the fleet, being sold to Leith owners in August 1899. Renamed DUNEARN she capsized on 26 August 1908 with a Japanese coal cargo for Singapore. There were only two survivors, picked up by the steamer SAIKIO MARU. Prior to her sale she had been in the news during April 1899. On passage from Iquique to Dunkirk with nitrate the propeller shaft fractured on 13 April. Soon after she was sighted by HERMES (99/3400gt) with wheat, cattle and sheep on R.P. Houston's service from the Plate to Liverpool. HERMES towed the casualty nearly 200 miles and three days later, despite the tow having parted on several occasions, left her anchored off Pernambuco. HERMES could not take her into port as she would have risked being refused permission to land her livestock in England. A month later AVERY HILL left in tow of the London tug OCEANA, discharged at Dunkirk and was towed on to Sunderland for repairs. Two days before AVERY HILL was sold the salvage award was announced by Mr Justice Barnes, HERMES received £2,200 for a job well performed. Soon after, DUNEARN towed the British India MOMBASA into Malta in heavy weather.

JUANITA NORTH was sold in January 1906 for £21,500 to become the Newcastle owned ELMSGARTH. She was sighted by Kapitänleutnant Victor Dieckmann of U61 on 29 September 1917 and torpedoed without loss of life 50 miles off Tory Island, while on passage from Matanzas with sugar for Liverpool. U61 survived another six months before she was sunk by PC51, there being no survivors.

As the fleet increased in the early years the issued capital steadily grew until the last of the authorised capital was issued in 1899. Results were good, a steady dividend of $7\frac{1}{2}\%$ being declared in each of the first four years. At the same time a steady policy of transferring funds to depreciation and reserves

ANGLO-AFRICAN (1). *(I.J. Farquhar Collection)*

was instituted, £42,000 in all during those first four years. This policy had been advocated by John Fleming, brother of the first chairman, who increased his shareholding when the policy was adopted.

In 1896 two further companies were floated. On 10 October the Southern Steam Shipping Company Ltd, controlled by the Short family, commenced business with a capital of £100,000 in £10 shares, followed on 17 December by the Seafield Shipping Company Ltd which had Lawther leanings with, initially, a capital of £35,000 in £5 shares. The Seafield capital was increased to £100,000 in November 1899.

Orders were placed in a steady stream. By the end of 1902 five more had joined the Nitrate Producers' fleet, and three each were commissioned for Southern and Seafield. ANGLO-CHILIAN, launched on 3 October 1898, introduced the nomenclature for which the fleet would become famous, the prefix ANGLO-, and the basis of the unofficial title "Anglo Line" seen in the shipping press. GEORGE FLEMING, SOUTH AFRICA and BLANEFIELD were sisters of JUANITA NORTH, three island steamers of 3400gt, 2200nt on dimensions of 353.0 x 45.0 x 17.2ft (25ft to spar deck). Machinery came either from Allan's Scotia Engine Works or George Clark and with two boilers working at 180 lb/sq in gave some 1500ihp and a speed of ten knots. ANGLO-CHILIAN in 1898 was a slightly larger, stretched version at 3800gt on a length of 369ft. Five can be divided into two groups, one of three island long bridge deck configuration, just over 4000gt, and the other with a combined bridge and forecastle, which increased their tonnage by approaching 200gt. ANGLO-AUSTRALIAN was the first long bridge decker to join the fleet, followed by SOUTH AUSTRALIA and WINKFIELD. With high bulwarks these long bridge deckers appeared, at a distance, to be flush decked. Captain Parsons transferred from the GEORGE FLEMING to ANGLO-AUSTRALIAN and reported that he considered she was not faster than the FLEMING, even though she was technically capable of twelve knots, as against ten of the older ship. The combined bridge and forecastle pair were SOUTH AMERICA and ANGLO-AFRICAN. All five had dimensions of 370.4 x 48.1 x 20.3ft (28.8ft to spar deck). More powerful machinery from Blair and Clark gave a speed of eleven to twelve knots. SOUTH AMERICA should have had machinery from Allan, but this was changed and she received an engine from Blair and Company: the Allan set of engines going into CEBRIANA owned by the Furness Withy controlled British Maritime Trust. Last came two slightly larger long bridge deckers, ANGLO-CANADIAN in October 1901 and ANGLO-SAXON in May 1902, with tonnages about 4250gt and a length of 380ft.

Henry Barnes took SOUTH AUSTRALIA when new, signing articles on 1 September 1899. Already aged 50, with many years at sea and a certificate of competency dated in London during 1873, Barnes later commissioned ANGLO-SAXON in 1902 before completing his seagoing career. Earlier SOUTH AFRICA had entered service under the command of George Dobson in November 1897. Dobson's previous command, for a year, had been the turret steamer TURRET COURT. The first of Doxford's turret ships, launched and named TURRET in November 1892, had been viewed with suspicion by owners and seamen alike. Commanded by Captain Petersen and managed by Petersen, Tate and Company, Newcastle, she had been followed by others. TURRET COURT had been commissioned in 1896 as the fourth of a series under the same management, designed to transit the Lachine Canal on the St Lawrence River. Even older than Barnes, having been born at Whitburn in 1830, Dobson transferred to SOUTH AMERICA in 1901 and remained with Latta until 1902, following which he joined Frank C. Strick and Company Ltd and took their AFGHANISTAN to sea.

From the beginning Latta was a strong believer in the importance of choosing a reliable and experienced master, and he quoted Samuel Lawther's dictum "Do not build a ship until you have secured a reliable captain, otherwise she will never do much good." One instance where this rule was clearly applied came in April 1899 when Frederick Parslow took command of GEORGE FLEMING. A Londoner born in 1856 Parslow had obtained his ticket in 1882 and between 1888 and 1899 was in command of Gulf Line ships. Gulf Line ran a service to the West Coast of South America, but increasingly became victim to poor financial management and a few years later were taken over by Furness, Withy and Company. In 1899 an arrangement started whereby F. and W. Ritson's Nautilus Steamship Company (Branch Line) placed their ships on the berth and in 1906 the Gulf Line rights were sold to Ritson. The 1899 change coincided with Captain Parslow joining the financially more healthy Anglo Line, with which he was to remain until his untimely death (see later). Commanding various of the fleet he took the ANGLO-

CALIFORNIAN new from the builders in 1912. Another Gulf Line master to join Lawther, Latta and Company was Herbert Golborne who transferred to take command of BLANEFIELD in July 1898. He left Latta in early 1904 when he signed on to command APHRODITE for Harris and Dixon, London.

Amongst officers who joined the company early in the 20th century, and whose names were to become well known on the West Coast of South America under the Nitrate Producers' flag, were Oswald Lewis and Walter Isaacs. Born in Kent, Lewis had served on ships managed by Cairns, Young and Noble, Newcastle, between 1896 and 1900. His first appointment was as mate on board ANGLO-AUSTRALIAN in August 1900, being promoted to command her in May 1902. Transferring to ANGLO-PATAGONIAN in 1910 he left the company in 1913, moving to Court Line, managed by Haldinstein and Company Ltd, London and their ERRINGTON COURT. Isaacs, born in 1871, had been with James Knott's Prince Line before signing on as mate of ANGLO-SAXON in April 1903, becoming master during February 1904. Like Lewis he later joined Court Line, taking their FRAMLINGTON COURT in 1911.

# BOOM AND RECESSION                                          *4*

The shipping market was buoyant in the closing years of the 19th century, illustrated at the third Annual General Meeting of the Seafield Shipping Company when a profit of over 60% of the capital was reported. War between China and Japan in 1894-5, followed by the Spanish-American War of 1898 and now, in October 1899, outbreak of hostilities in South Africa saw demand brisk. The South African War, or Boer War, was to see large numbers of British ships taken on charter to not only move British and Colonial troops to the scene of action from all parts of the Empire, but then to keep them supplied. In 1900 the Boxer Rising in China added to the number of ships needed in Government service.

The emergency in South Africa required, up to the end of March 1902, the services of over five million tons of shipping which made 904 passages to the colony and carried 366,821 men, 304,791 horses and 99,378 mules as well as stores, munitions and supplies for the armed forces there. By the end of the war 380,000 men, 460,000 animals and over a million tons of supplies had been shipped, making the South African War the greatest campaign fought overseas by British forces, surpassing the Crimea, Wellington's Peninsula Campaign and others. In 1914 a war commenced that was sadly to eclipse it.

Lawther, Latta and Company were heavily involved, eleven of the fleet being engaged in the work and making 34 passages with troops, horses, mules and supplies, several being taken up newly completed from the shipyards. From the list of charters it will be seen two passages, by WINKFIELD, were as troop transports with yeomanry troops and their horses, another twelve were

*Transport Medal,*
*1899-1902*

as horse transports, six with mules and fourteen carrying supplies. The spar deck ships were of particular value as transports for men and animals, as well as stores.

For the first time ever, a special silver medal, The Transport Medal 1899-1902, was introduced for the Mercantile Marine but awarded only to masters and officers of troop transports and hospital ships employed to South Africa and China. The reverse depicted the Orient Line OPHIR. WINKFIELD was the sole ship in the fleet of Lawther, Latta and Company to qualify and Captain Golborne and his officers duly received their medals. Robert Lawther was one of the twenty nine representatives of companies supplying the transports who received invitations to be present at Buckingham Palace when King Edward VII distributed the medals on 4 November 1903, after which they were presented to His Majesty. The only other exclusively Mercantile Marine medal issued is the Mercantile Marine War Medal 1914-1918. This bronze medal was, however, awarded to all ranks meeting the service requirements and over 133,000 were issued as compared with less than 1,800 of the Transport Medal.

In early April 1900 the latest addition to the fleet, Seafield's WINKFIELD, was in the news. Completing trials on 24 February she proceeded to London to embark 322 officers and men, also 241 horses, of the Northumberland Yeomanry. Sailing on 13 March she was nearing the end of the passage to Cape Town when, on 4 April, she ran into dense fog some 70 miles off Cape Town. As she reduced speed the Union Line's MEXICAN, running at half speed, loomed out of the fog. Despite helm and engine manoeuvres to try and avoid collision this was impossible and WINKFIELD hit MEXICAN on the port side of her engine room. Passengers and crew were transferred from MEXICAN to WINKFIELD and the troopship MONTROSE which arrived shortly after. WINKFIELD took MEXICAN in tow but had to slip it and proceed to Cape Town where MEXICAN's passengers were transferred, mainly to GUELPH which sailed two days later for England. The day after the collision TAGUS could only find wreckage where MEXICAN had finally sunk. The Court of Inquiry in Cape Town found neither ship to blame.

In 1901 the freight market started to collapse. Ships taken on charter for South Africa in 1899-1900 at a lump sum of £8,000 to 9,000 were now being taken up at £5,000 to £5,500 and in 1902 the figures had further tumbled to £3,500 to £4,500. From October 1899 to September 1902 rates varied between 15s and 35s per gross ton, with an average of 18s 3d. This pattern, so far as it applied to the fleets managed by Lawther, Latta and Company, can be seen in the table of Boer War charters. The Government White Papers detailing all ships chartered for South Africa and China during the period confirms the collapse of the market on a wider scale. John Latta and Robert Lawther had felt pessimistic about the market keeping up and fixed as many charters ahead as possible in 1901, thus alleviating the consequences for the company.

**Boer War charters—1899-1902**

ANGLO-AFRICAN
1. London 25.11.00 to Cape Town 20.12.00. £8,500.
2. Montreal 22.5.01 to Cape Town 18.6.01. 750 horses.
3. Queenstown 23.2.02 to Cape Town 19.3.02. 503 horses.
ANGLO-AUSTRALIAN
1. London 4.2.00 to Cape Town 5.3.00. £8,000.
2. New Orleans 19.9.00 to Cape Town 23.10.00. 1301 mules.
3. New Orleans 9.4.01 to Cape Town 11.5.01. 1002 mules.
ANGLO-CANADIAN
1. Fiume 6.11.01 to Cape Town 29.11.01. 800 mules.
2. Fiume 6.1.02 to Cape Town 2.2.02. 800 mules.
3. Fiume 27.3.02 to Cape Town 23.4.02. 800 mules.
ANGLO-CHILIAN
1. London 20.12.99 to Cape Town 13.1.00. £9,000.
2. Gibraltar 28.6.00 to Cape Town 20.7.00. 825 mules.
3. Queenstown 10.3.01 to Cape Town 21.4.01. 550 horses. £5,500.
4. New Orleans 30.9.01 to Cape Town 2.11.01. 850 mules.
5. London 1.5.02 to Cape Town 25.5.02. £4,500.
ANGLO-SAXON
1. Fiume 22.6.02 to Cape Town 18.7.02.
BLANEFIELD
1. London 8.12.00 to Cape Town 4.1.01. £8,000.
2. London 4.11.01 to Cape Town 11.12.01. £5,250.
3. London 26.4.02 to Cape Town 26.5.02. £3,500.
GEORGE FLEMING
1. London 18.11.00 to Cape Town 18.12.00. £8,000.
2. London 15.12.01 to Cape Town 15.1.02. £4,600.
JUANITA NORTH
1. London 25.12.00 to Cape Town 21.1.01. £8,000.
2. London 1.9.01 to Cape Town 28.9.01. £5,500.
3. London 26.6.02 to Cape Town 24.7.02. £4,400.
SOUTH AMERICA
1. New Orleans 14.4.01 to Cape Town 11.5.01. 1000 mules.
SOUTH AUSTRALIA
1. London 10.4.00 to Cape Town 10.5.00. £8,500.
2. Queenstown 28.3.01 to Cape Town 21.4.01. 550 horses.
3. Queenstown 16.1.02 to Cape Town 10.2.02. 550 horses.
4. Fiume 31.3.02 to Cape Town 29.4.02. 750 horses.
WINKFIELD
1. London 13.3.00 to Cape Town 6.4.00. 322 troops, 241 horses.
2. London 27.7.00 to Cape Town 20.8.00. 264 troops, 247 horses.
3. Queenstown 23.4.01 to Cape Town 16.5.01. 500 horses.
                Charter £22,884 for these three passages.
4. New Orleans 15.11.00 to Cape Town 17.12.00. 1233 mules.
5. Melbourne 6.11.01 to Cape Town 7.1.02. 300 horses.
6. Queenstown 3.3.02 to Cape Town 27.3.02. 496 horses.
Notes. — Each passage gives sailing port and date, arrival port and date. Numbers of troops, horses and mules and charter price if known. Invariably the ships sailed to Cape Town for orders and went on to another port, such as East London, Delagoa Bay, Algoa Bay, &c, to discharge.

The British Government had purchased large numbers of remounts, draft and butchery animals from many countries to keep the Imperial army mobile in action against the Boers, as well as fed. One country to ship large numbers of livestock was Argentina, and after the war ended Lawther, Latta and Company obtained a two year contract to restock the country with stud cattle, sheep and donkeys.

After the 6th annual report to Nitrate Producers' shareholders rumour spread

WINKFIELD, chartered as troopship 99, sailing down the Thames with the Northumberland Yeomanry bound for the Boer War. The bow tug, Elliott Steam Tug Co's CHAMPION (built 1892, 116gt, broken up 1936), is flying the burgee of Lawther, Latta & Co. and the houseflag of WINKFIELD's owners, the Seafield Shipping Co. Ltd.

(Painting by C. Cockerhan; Courtesy Sunderland Museum and Art Gallery — Tyne & Wear Museums)

round the London market that the affairs of the company had so impressed an American investor he was offering £550,000 for the fleet of nine ships owned by the three companies, management to remain with Lawther, Latta and Company. This offer compares with a new cost of just over £400,000, which had been depreciated in the accounts to about £210,000, allied with corresponding investments and reserves. The offer was declined and a figure £50,000 higher suggested, but the potential buyer did not respond to this counter offer.

During 1901 John Latta first spoke and complained of the Suez Canal handling of the rating of shelter deckers, as the spar deck design was loosely termed (Nitrate Producers' were not to commission their first true shelter decker until 1905). As one of the first builders of the type, Lawther, Latta and Company had been assured by the Board of Trade that canal charges would not be levied on the shelter deck unless it was occupied by cargo. At first this proved to be true, but then, to quote "Fairplay" for 11 July 1901 —

"The (Suez Canal) Company has observed that the ends of the shelter-decks on the large modern boats are pierced with rivet-holes, so that the spaces can be closed up when filled with cargo, and on the strength of this the Company is claiming dues on the space when it contains no cargo."

Citing the Canal Regulations of 1873 as authority, regulations which did not anticipate this design of ship, the Suez Canal Company now commenced collecting dues on all spaces where cargo may once have been carried. Latta cited a single deck collier with 6,000 tons of coal as having to pay £300 less than one of his shelter deck vessels with a similar cargo. He had therefore to refuse several cargoes which he would otherwise have taken, and at times found it cheaper to dispatch ships via the Cape than take the Suez route.

The Nitrate Producers' houseflag was first seen in Australia in early November 1897 when GEORGE FLEMING, named after the first chairman, arrived at Port Pirie from New York on her maiden voyage. Soon ships were being placed on the wool berth to load for the United Kingdom. George Wills and Company, Adelaide, John Sanderson and Company, Melbourne, and Gilchrist, Watt and Sanderson Ltd, Sydney, had formed "The Syndicate" to work together loading weekly ships during the wool season from June to February. Most of the ships were supplied by Holt's Blue Funnel and Lund's Blue Anchor Lines, but Lawther, Latta and Company provided a few ships. In the 1901-1902 season the programme was sent to London with four positions open and it was arranged ANGLO-AFRICAN should fill position 12 and ANGLO-CHILIAN the 18th. ANGLO-CHILIAN was scheduled to arrive at Sydney on 17 December but being detained in South America Wills arranged for WINCHESTER to take the berth. When WINCHESTER in her turn was delayed ESKDALE was put on. WINCHESTER was ready to load on 17 December, the last wool sales before Christmas took place the following day and she sailed on Christmas Eve. ANGLO-CHILIAN arrived on 20 December and had to wait for the January sales, being detained and getting away on 28 January with a part cargo of wool, topped up with grain. Lawther, Latta and Company took George Wills and Company to court contending they had not been advised of the extra two ships arranged and seeking to recover £4,299 in respect of the detention of ANGLO-CHILIAN. Mr Justice Kennedy found in favour of ANGLO-CHILIAN in July 1903, only to have the decision reversed on appeal by the Master of the Rolls.

The pattern of trade can be seen from a examination of just one issue of Lloyd's Weekly Index in 1903 —

| Position Report—5 March 1903 |
| --- |
| ANGLO-AFRICAN—arrived Port Natal 1 February from Buenos Ayres. |
| ANGLO-AUSTRALIAN—arrived Buenos Ayres 19 February from Port Natal. |
| ANGLO-CANADIAN—sailed Melbourne 31 January for London. |
| ANGLO-CHILIAN—sailed East London 3 March for Montevideo. |
| ANGLO-SAXON—passed Las Palmas 27 February, Arica for Dunkirk (arrived 7 March). |
| BLANEFIELD—sailed Antofagasta 22 January for Callao. |
| GEORGE FLEMING—at Barry loading for Antofagasta (sailed 5 March). |
| JUANITA NORTH—arrived Buenos Ayres 9 February from Port Natal. |
| SOUTH AMERICA—sailed Mollendo 22 February for Buenos Ayres and Table Bay. |
| SOUTH AUSTRALIA—arrived Buenos Ayres 14 February from Delagoa Bay. |
| WINKFIELD—sailed Buenos Ayres 25 February for Table Bay. |

With the bad shipping market it was to be 1905 before the next ship was commissioned for any of the companies. SOUTH AFRICA had been sold in April 1900, to Spanish interests as NEPTUNO only to founder in the Bay of Biscay on 25 November 1902 with the loss of most of her crew. Five survivors were picked up from a lifeboat by the barque BRYNYMOR (Barry for Algoa Bay, coal) which put back with heavy weather damage sustained in the Bay.

The companies finished the Boer War with a fleet of ten ships which number remained constant for some years. This could have proved otherwise as WINKFIELD had a spectacular casualty in 1902 from which she escaped unscathed. Having arrived at Manchester on 5 December from Savannah she discharged a part cargo of cotton before moving to Runcorn to land 1600 tons of phosphate rock. Proceeding down the Ship Canal she entered the large (600ft by 65ft) lock at Barton with the tug FLYING BREEZE as bow tug. The pilot rang for astern, the linkage of the engine room telegraph snapped and the repeater went to ahead. Not knowing what had happened the engineer obeyed the telegraph and she surged ahead through the lock. The crew of FLYING BREEZE saw her coming and were able to leap to safety before their ship was run down and sunk. WINKFIELD then hit the lower lock gates, tore them off their hinges and dropped 15ft into the lower section of the canal. Behind her the top gates were closing when the rush of water rammed them together and caused some damage. Fortunately they held. It was five days before the locks were returned to service. The tug was lifted and scrapped, the intermediate gates in the lock were closed to enable repairs to be made to the upper gates and were then lifted and moved to the lower end whilst those damaged gates were recovered and repaired. These repairs to the lock gates and the loss of FLYING BREEZE added up to a claim for £17,504. Smaller vessels were able to continue using the smaller (350ft by 45ft) lock but larger vessels such as MANCHESTER SHIPPER had to be handled lower down the canal until the large lock reopened.

Prior to the Manchester Ship Canal opening in 1894 experts had predicted such accidents could never happen, but HAROLD (91/682gt) had disproved that when she went through Latchford 65ft lock on 10 April 1895, followed by STARLIGHT (84/1481gt) at the Barton 65ft lock on 24 November 1899. WINKFIELD, also at Barton Lock, was the third such accident to be recorded. But the strangest such incident must have been early in July 1906 when CASSIA (83/1088gt), bound for Manchester with ore from Pomaron, swerved when making for the 45ft lock at Irlam and struck the lower gates of the 65ft lock. The large lock was ready to receive CHERENOA (97/3203gt) coming down canal. CASSIA drove the lock gates back against the 16ft head of water and lifted them from their hinges, the intermediate gates were displaced by water pressure and the top gates were damaged as they crashed together in the rush of water through the lock.

Lawther, Latta and Company continued to develop their integrated shipping and trading interests, being agents for both Westport (New Zealand) and Lota (Chilean) coal. A normal pattern of trade for many of the ships was to load a mixed cargo for Chile, topping up with coal, then nitrates north to the United States and return to Europe with cotton and other cargo. Coal was the energy source for most of world industry, the intrusion of oil hardly noticed. For many years Britain had been the largest producer, only recently overtaken by the U.S.A. In 1913 sales of coal in Britain for export and bunkers topped 94 million tons before a steady decline set in between the wars, 80 million tons in 1924, 53 million in 1933 and 46 million in 1938. During 1904 Chile mined 750,000 tons of soft coal and imported 914,000 tons (446,000 from the United Kingdom, 457,000 from Australia and 11,000 from the United States). British and Australian coal fuelled the nitrate oficinas, although increasingly oil was being adopted.

Amongst charters undertaken were some to Charles G. Dunn and Company Ltd, Liverpool, managers of the New York and South America Line operating from New York to the West Coast of South America. The design of the Anglo Line fleet and the experience of their masters and crews were a great attraction, and these charters in no way competed with their own run from Europe. On the outbreak of war in 1914 Dunn's fleet of five steamers, also the London based Isthmian Steamship Company Ltd's five vessels, were sold to United States Steel Products Company Inc, New York, and later were well known as the Isthmian Line. This transfer would indicate their true ownership lay in the United States, with the Red Ensign employed as a flag of convenience. Other British flag fleets which underwent similar reflagging included those of W.R. Grace and Company, New York, and the United Fruit Company, Boston.

ANGLO-PERUVIAN, launched on 3 August 1905, was the first true shelter decker to join the fleet. The earlier spar deck was too light to be counted as part of the hull structure for freeboard purposes but with heavier scantlings it could now become a shelter deck and be included in those calculations. She was also the first of the fleet to be fitted with quadruple expansion machinery. Lawther, Latta and Company were one of only two British cargo

*Robert Lawther outside the family home (Mount Vernon, Belfast) with his new car, a single cylinder 6hp De Dion voiturette. Samuel Lawther stands on the steps behind.*
*(D. Briggs)*

ship fleets to adopt this machinery extensively, the other being the London based New York and Pacific Steamship Company Ltd, commencing with their CHARCAS of 1906. ANGLO-PERUVIAN had only a short career, she made one trip to Valparaiso and Tocopilla and was outward bound on her second voyage, from the Tyne on passage for Philadelphia with 3,000 tons of coal as ballast, when she hit an iceberg on 21 April 1906. Three days later the steamer MOHAWK took off her crew before she foundered, landing all 38 at Weymouth. In command of ANGLO-PERUVIAN was Wilson Curtis who had joined Latta as mate of BLANEFIELD in July 1898, taking command in November 1899. He remained with BLANEFIELD until taking the new ANGLO-PERUVIAN to sea in October 1905. Following her loss he left the company, as often happened in many companies when a master lost his ship in casualty, his next ship, and last command, being BALLOCHMYLE until he left the sea in 1908.

The New York and Pacific Steamship Company, operators of the Merchants' Line from New York to ports in Ecuador, Peru and Chile, was owned by W.R. Grace and Company, New York, another business built on South American enterprise. William Russell Grace was an Irishman born at Queenstown in 1832 who had, with his brother, developed a trading firm at Callao, Peru. In 1865 he organised W.R. Grace and Company in New York to act as correspondents for the Peruvian Government. On the other side of the 1879 war from North he had supplied much of the equipment and munitions needed by the Peruvian forces, and after their defeat was instrumental in financing the Peruvian national debt. Receiving huge concessions for these services he

31

went on to build a major trading, banking and shipping empire, using the Red Ensign as a flag of convenience for his fleet.

In 1905 fleet renewal commenced as a matter of policy, although the freight returns were still very low. "Fairplay" summarised the earnings per ton deadweight for the fleet. These figures well illustrate the condition of the market with 1909 earnings reaching a low of 21% of those achieved in 1901. ANGLO-PERUVIAN of 1905 was followed at yearly intervals by ANGLO-BOLIVIAN, ANGLO-COLOMBIAN and ANGLO-MEXICAN. The first pair were the largest ships in the fleet at 5,500gt on dimensions of 418 x 54 x 29ft. ANGLO-PERUVIAN had machinery supplied by Gray's Central Marine Engine Works at Hartlepool, whereas her sister ANGLO-BOLIVIAN, launched in October 1906, took engines from the North Eastern Marine Engineering Company, who were to be preferred suppliers for many years to come. The 1907-1908 sisters were slightly smaller at 394.8 x 52.5 x 27.9ft with a tonnage of 4795gt. Also engined by North Eastern Marine they produced 2700ihp against the 3000ihp of the larger pair. All had three boilers pressed to 220 lb/sq in and were eleven knotters.

| Earnings per ton deadweight from freight and investments | | | | | |
|---|---|---|---|---|---|
| | Years ending 30 April. 1901 taken as 100%. | | | | |
| 1898 | £1. 3. 0d. | 47.58% | 1915 | £1.13.10d. | 70.--% |
| 1899 | 1.12. 1. | 66.37 | 1916 | 4.17. 6. | 203.12 |
| 1900 | 1. 5. 9. | 53.24 | 1917 | 3.13. 9. | 159.88 |
| 1901 | 2. 8. 0. | 100.-- | 1918 | 3. 0. 9. | 126.56 |
| 1902 | 1. 7. 2. | 56.20 | 1919 | 3. 6. 5. | 138.19 |
| 1903 | 18. 6. | 38.27 | 1920 | 3. 0. 0. | 125.-- |
| 1904 | 12. 3. | 25.34 | 1921 | 2. 6. 5. | 96.70 |
| 1905 | 14. 5. | 29.82 | 1922 | 2. 1. 7. | 86.63 |
| 1906 | 12. 2. | 25.24 | 1923 | 18. 6. | 38.54 |
| 1907 | 11. 0. | 22.75 | 1924 | 15. 4. | 31.94 |
| 1908 | 12. 0. | 24.82 | 1925 | 1. 1. 4. | 44.44 |
| 1909 | 10. 2. | 21.03 | 1926 | 18. 8. | 38.88 |
| 1910 | 12. 3. | 25.34 | 1927 | 1.12. 8. | 68.05 |
| 1911 | 14. 6. | 30.-- | 1928 | 1.18.10. | 80.90 |
| 1912 | 17.10. | 36.72 | 1929 | 1. 8.11. | 60.24 |
| 1913 | 1.18. 1. | 78.79 | 1930 | 1. 3. 3. | 48.44 |
| 1914 | 1.10. 2. | 62.41 | | | |

During 1907 Latta turned his mind to the amalgamation of the three companies. It was not straight forward as the assets varied so greatly. Whereas Nitrate Producers' had reserves amounting to 90% of their capital, the other two, Southern and Seafield, had only 50% reserves. This problem was overcome and in November the fusion took place with an exchange of shares, after which both Southern and Seafield were wound up.

That same year, 1907, Latta promoted Percival Greenhill to command of GEORGE FLEMING. Greenhill had passed for his 'ticket' in 1903 and been appointed mate of that vessel. He was to remain with Latta nearly to the end, apart from a short period in 1918 when he took WAR FIRTH and WAR WASP for J. Chadwick and Sons, signing off ANGLO-CANADIAN in November 1941. In 1946 Captain Greenhill was appointed to be an Officer of the Most Excellent Order of the British Empire (OBE) for war services.

Robert Lawther and John Latta were involved at this time in a rather different venture. Following the discovery of gold in the Yukon during August 1896 the Rush of optimistic prospectors that followed highlighted the complete lack of communications in the area. Most prospectors went by sea to Skagway, hiked 45 miles over the trails through the White Pass or Chilkoot Pass to reach the Yukon River, down which they floated 500 miles to Dawson City and the gold creeks. During 1899 the opening of the White Pass and Yukon Railway eased the privation of the trails and connected Skagway with Whitehorse on the Yukon River, from which point river steamers operated to Dawson City in the summer months. Meanwhile at Dawson City the Klondike Mines Railway was promoted to act as a distributor from that point, to run for 84 miles to Stewart River.

Lawther and Latta's introduction to the Klondike is not now known, but from their long association with A.N.C. Treadgold (1863-1950) it is possible they were early introduced to this schoolmaster turned gold prospector and company promoter. After eleven years as a teacher Treadgold had left the faculty at Bath College to embark on the ETRURIA for New York early in January 1898, from whence he crossed the continent and reached Dawson City early in June 1898. Rather than concentrate on pick and shovel gold mining he toured the fields and developed his scheme for large scale extraction using dredges to recover the gold bearing gravel, supported by water and electricity supply schemes. In his novel "Burning Daylight", Jack London promotes this style of working. Although it is not known if London knew Treadgold, they definitely had mutual acquaintances and friends.

For such a large scale scheme to work consolidation of the individual claims was vital, and Treadgold worked steadily to achieve this. Interesting the Guggenheim family in the investment potential, the Yukon Gold Company was formed in 1906 to work Bonanza Creek. Treadgold sold his interest in this venture in 1908 to develop wider consolidation plans for the rest of the Klondike. Starting with the Granville Mining Company in 1911 this developed until finally 1923 saw the formation of the Yukon Consolidated Gold Corporation which, a few years later, absorbed the Yukon Gold Company to achieve the total consolidation dreams of Treadgold.

Sadly Treadgold, although a man of vision, was a thoroughly incompetent manager in the field, and this led to dispute and court action by shareholders to stop his disastrous management methods and stop the Corporation collapsing. In this dispute, which dragged on for many years, Lawther and Latta found themselves amongst those shareholders opposed to Treadgold, rather than supporting his actions as previously.

*Klondike Mines Railway train passing Yukon Gold Co's Dredge YUKON NO 1 at Bonanza Creek, 1908. (Dawson City Museum & Historical Society)*

Lawther and Latta originally chose to invest in the Klondike by taking an important role in the development of local transport. The Dawson, Grand Forks and Stewart River Railway Corporation Ltd was floated in London during 1904 to raise British finance to construct the Klondike Mines Railway, Lawther having obtained the contract to construct the first section of 15 miles from Dawson City to Grand Falls. The commission on this contract was £10,000, taken as shares in the Corporation (in fact the total ordinary share capital). The finance to construct the line was raised by the issue of debentures, £50,000 Prior Lien 6% and £225,000 Consolidated 6%. The Corporation received bonds, certificates of indebtedness and common stock from the railway in payment for the line.

Construction had commenced in 1903 and been abandoned until 1905. By the following year much of the trackbed to Grand Falls was complete, some rails laid and others ready on the ground. Piers for bridges over the Klondike River were up and some of the steelwork erected, whilst rolling stock was ready at Klondike City and White Horse. Robert Lawther visited the line in June 1907 and again in September 1908, reporting optimistically on the traffic potential.

The first traffic moved in May 1906 on the line to Grand Falls whilst the extension to Sulphur Springs opened to traffic on 5 November 1906 at a total cost of $884,804.69 for the 31 miles, the remote site and the gold rush location resulting in the bill being far greater than a similar line anywhere else in the world. The total cost to Stewart River had been estimated in 1903 at $2,556,784.

Projected traffic and receipts anticipated a healthy surplus but in the first few years traffic failed to meet these optimistic expectations and by the end of May 1908 losses of $121,596.65 had accrued. Conditions had changed since the days of the Rush, mining had changed from the individual panning for placer gold to large companies operating gold dredgers. The number of people in the district had fallen, from a peak of 30,000 people Dawson City dwindled

34

to 3,000 in 1912 and in 1941 was officially listed as 1,000. With this the number of passengers and volume of freight traffic dissipated.

Needless to say the extension to Stewart River was never built. In London interest payments on the Prior Lien Debentures were suspended in 1911 and the annual accounts for the year ending October 1914 show the £275,000 debentures had accrued unpaid interest totalling £118,750.

The railway suddenly ceased running in July 1914, leaving the $2,171,250 of bonds and stock held as security by the Corporation virtually worthless. In February 1916 the decision was taken to place the Dawson, Grand Forks and Stewart River Railway Corporation Ltd in voluntary liquidation as the chance of recovering anything from the assets in the remote reaches of the Yukon was small. Interestingly all four locomotives owned, left in the Yukon on closure, were to survive into the preservation era and are still in existence.

Although this was the end of the railway both Lawther and Latta retained lifelong interest and investment in the Klondike, whilst from his father's long association with trade from Canada to Northern Ireland Lawther also held other business interests in the Dominion. As has been mentioned, to the end of their lives both men were concerned in the recovery of Klondike gold by the Yukon Consolidated Gold Corporation.

Robert Lawther retired from day-to-day business in London during 1911, although he retained an active interest in both the London firm, the Lawther interests in Ireland and investments in Canada and elsewhere. He continued to live in London and the South of England until after the death of his brother in 1929, then returning to the family home in Belfast, Mount Vernon. In 1912 John Latta had a narrow escape: one evening in November he was, with his wife, involved in a serious motoring accident in Hyde Park. En route to a dinner party in Kensington their motor car was in collision with one owned by Mr Jessel, KC. Latta was thrown through the front glass and his scalp lacerated. Mrs Latta fell to the bottom of the car, suffering severe shock. Their chauffeur was saved by the steering wheel bending right forward through the glass screen whilst their footman was thrown to the ground and sustained bruises. The sole occupant of Mr Jessel's car, the chauffeur, escaped injury. Mr Latta was taken to St Mary's Hospital and returned home in the early hours of the following morning.

From 1906 to 1913 seven of the fleet were lost or sold and five new ships ordered from 1910 until the outbreak of World War I in 1914. In the early hours of 1 May 1906 BLANEFIELD, on passage from Junin for Dover, where orders giving her discharge port for the nitrate cargo would be communicated through Lloyd's Signal Station, was lost in collision off Beachy Head, run down by the 4-masted barque KATE THOMAS. This loss had an adverse effect on insurance premium rates for nitrate cargo as several ships had been lost, such as CLYDESDALE on fire at Tocopilla and sunk in December 1903, W.J. PIRRIE burnt at Tocopilla in August 1904, PENGWERN wrecked off Cuxhaven in January 1907 and ORMSARY so long overdue that her reinsurance on the overdue market against total loss only reached 90 guineas percent.

*Her foremast falling, RELIANCE on fire at Iquique in 1901.*
*(National Maritime Museum)*

Fire was one of the greatest dangers with nitrate cargo. Using water as an extinguisher on such cargo was useless, only water which had nitrate soaking in it worked. Hence, whilst loading, barrels of nitrate-water were kept alongside each hatch. This risk was well appreciated in the light of many fire losses. In addition to the casualties mentioned there were others, such as MICRONESIA on fire nearing the end of her passage from Iquique for Ostend in June 1897. Beached near Deal she was later refloated, underwriters agreed a compromised total loss of $97\frac{1}{2}\%$ and she was sold for breaking up. Losses by fire whilst loading included ROSS-SHIRE at Pisagua in December 1900, RELIANCE at Iquique in September 1901 and DUNS LAW, again at Iquique, in December 1904. Robert Lawther would have particularly noted W.J. PIRRIE at Tocopilla in August 1904, although she was no longer owned and managed by his father. Between 1891 and 1914 "Lloyd's List" reported 23 nitrate laden ships lost by fire, 17 of which casualties occurred whilst loading at Chilean ports.

---

**Ships burnt loading nitrate—1891-1914**

Pisagua—SEA QUEEN 16 April 1891: ROSS-SHIRE 24 December 1900.
Iquique—CHILE 11 September 1892: MELPOMENE 6 June 1894: ARCTURUS 11 November 1895: MARION BALLANTYNE 6 December 1900: RELIANCE 12 September 1901: DUNS LAW 26 December 1904: BISMARCK 18 November 1909: MARION FRAZER 10 October 1910.
Junin—WILLIAM W. CRAPO 3 July 1895: ICEBERG 18 November 1895.
Tocopilla—JOHN O'GAUNT 24 January 1897: CLYDESDALE 10 December 1903: W.J. PIRRIE 18 August 1904.
Antofagasta—POSEIDON 22 December 1907: NAUARCHOS 17 April 1908.

---

Early in February 1902 the Committee of Lloyd's approved a letter drafted by Lloyd's Agent at Iquique, following the burning of MARION BALLANTYNE and RELIANCE, to be handed to the masters of all English vessels arriving to load nitrate. It advised the covering of all hatches as soon as the day's work was over, and avoiding exposure of nitrate in bags on deck where a spark from the donkey boiler, galley or someone's pipe could start a conflagration. Such exposure stemmed from the common practice of making loading stages from piles of bagged nitrate, which burned easily when in bags.

Many years later the cause of such fires was established. Losses of nitrate laden ships continued to feature in the loss returns prepared by Lloyd's Register of Shipping. Then the Norwegian motorship GISLA (24/3549gt) caught fire on 21 February 1936, whilst discharging nitrate from Valparaiso at Pier 8,

Baltimore. Captain Ebbesen had gone ashore earlier in the day and learnt from newspapers that a ship was on fire, little realising it was his own vessel. She sank the following day following an explosion. Although only twelve years old, when refloated on 2 March the damage was so extensive she was condemned and broken up. The Bureau of Marine Inspection and Navigation joined with the Bureau of Mines, the Bureau of Standards and the Chilean Nitrate Sales Corporation to study the problem, the peculiarly self-sustaining character of nitrate fires. It was established that sodium nitrate was not an explosive and did not burn in the ordinary sense, but when heated over 700°F nitrate decomposes and gives off oxygen. Invariably nitrate fires started in bagged, not bulk, cargo, often due to a cigarette or match igniting a jute and paper bag. Once heat built up the dangerous property of nitrate became apparent, as the nitrate in contact with the flame decomposed and oxygen fed the fire. Shutting off draughts, using foam or other extinguishing methods had little or no effect on the conflagration, which spread through the bags into wooden dunnage and cargo battens until all inflammable or carboniferous material had been consumed. The only cure for nitrate fires was prevention, enforcing no smoking rules and ensuring no source of fire was allowed near the cargo.

ANGLO-AFRICAN was wrecked on 7 January 1909 in fog four miles south of Cape Charles as she neared the end of a passage from Tocopilla for Baltimore with nitrate valued at £71,300. Within a couple of days she had become a total loss. The Court of Inquiry considered Captain James Henderson failed to take sufficient care in ascertaining his position in the prevailing conditions and suspended his certificate for three months. SOUTH AMERICA was another fog casualty. On the most profitable charter she had ever had, to the Hamburg America Line, she was on a ballast passage from Hamburg for Cardiff when, on 13 March 1912, she went on to the rocks at St Loy in fog, six miles west of Penzance. Passing down Channel the thick weather cleared for a spell. But half an hour after signalling "All's Well" to the Lloyd's Signal Station at the Lizard fog and drizzle returned and, at midnight, course was altered to round Land's End. The Inquiry censured Captain Alfred Bowling for altering course from WNW to NWbyW without taking more care and using the lead as, with shore lights obscured, the set of the wind, tide and current, the ship was being set in towards the land. The crew landed using their own boats, the salvage vessel LADY OF THE ISLES attended, but with extensive bottom damage salvage was not feasible and underwriters disposed of the wreck to the Western Marine Salvage Company, Penzance, who broke her up on the spot. Seven months later the French steamer ABERTAY (88/1088gt) came ashore alongside her and also became a total loss. Initially the French captain believed he had been in collision as he lay so close alongside SOUTH AMERICA.

Sales included GEORGE FLEMING and ANGLO-CHILIAN in 1911, WINKFIELD the following year and SOUTH AUSTRALIA in 1913. GEORGE FLEMING became the Italian AFFINITA until broken up in 1932, ANGLO-CHILIAN was renamed RIO IGUASSU under the control of Petersen

*ANGLO-MEXICAN* *(World Ship Photo Library)*

and Company, London. Ships were not the only thing to pass to Petersen and Company, Captain Freemantle left ANGLO-AUSTRALIAN in November 1911 and took Petersen's RIO SOROCABA the following year. Owen Freemantle had been with Furness, Withy and Company, rising to command LONDON CITY before joining Latta's SOUTH AMERICA as mate in the summer of 1904. He remained with Petersen through World War I and finally retired from the sea in February 1933. Meanwhile RIO IGUASSU had been captured and sunk by the German light cruiser SMS KARLSRUHE on 22 September 1914 whilst carrying coal from the Tyne for Rio de Janeiro. Her crew joined seamen from many other ships sunk by KARLSRUHE, including STRATHROY, MAPLE BRANCH, HIGHLAND HOPE, INDRANI, CORNISH CITY, NICETO DE LARRINAGA, LYNROWAN, CERVANTES, PRUTH and CONDOR on board the German steamer CREFELD which landed them at Teneriffe on 22 October, from whence they were repatriated on the LA ROSARINA and ANDORINHA, landing at Liverpool on 3 November. WINKFIELD became the Russian SADKO and was broken up in 1926 whilst SOUTH AUSTRALIA also went to Petersen and Company as RIO BLANCO. Passing to Spanish interests during 1920 and renamed PEPITO MUMBRO she only lasted eighteen months until wrecked off Abo on passage from Petrograd for the Tyne in ballast. SOUTH AUSTRALIA had nearly been sold late in 1907 when the offer by W.J. Tatem and Company to buy the Short Brothers built SAGAMI fell through. A near sister to SOUTH AUSTRALIA, Tatem were offered her instead but declined as she was too old. SAGAMI had been built in 1902, as against 1899 for SOUTH AUSTRALIA.

At the Annual General Meeting in 1910 John Latta had the sad task of reporting the deaths of four men closely connected with the venture. Vice-Admiral Sir George Boyes had been a director of the Seafield Shipping

Company until appointed Director of Transports, Colonel Church was an original shareholder, John Fleming, brother of the first chairman and Vice-Admiral Orford Churchill whose son, Sub-Lieutenant John Churchill, had been lost in the first Royal Navy submarine loss, when A1 sank in March 1904. Two years later a fellow director, Sir Theodore Fry, died.

*ANGLO-EGYPTIAN at Adelaide*                                    *(I.J. Farquhar Collection)*

The new tonnage commissioned from 1910 on exhibited the latest technology. First came ANGLO-PATAGONIAN launched on 26 May 1910, the third ship in the fleet to exceed 5,000gt. She was, more importantly, the first Isherwood longitudinally framed ship constructed on the Wear. Joseph Isherwood (1870-1937) had joined the West Hartlepool shipyard of Edward Withy and Company in 1886 and trained as a draughtsman. Leaving in 1896 he became a surveyor with Lloyd's Register of Shipping and whilst so employed explored the science of ship construction in relation to strength. This led to his evolving and patenting the longitudinal system of framing. He left Lloyd's Register in 1907 and established his own design office. The first ship built to the system was the tanker PAUL PAIX completed in November 1908, followed by McIver's GASCONY three months later. ANGLO-PATAGONIAN was the ninth to be launched in the United Kingdom and was the first of a series for Nitrate Producers'. Her delivery was delayed due to a cracked cylinder. Regrettably, her career was cut short on 10 July 1917 when torpedoed by Oberleutnant Ernst Voigt of UC72 as she neared the French coast on passage from New York for Bordeaux with horses and a general cargo.

The wreck of ANGLO-PATAGONIAN was located in 1930 by the Italian salvage steamer ROSTRO which recovered some 553 tons of steel, brass and copper. ROSTRO was owned by Societa Ricuperi Marittimi (SORIMA), Genoa, a company famous for the recovery of bullion from the P & O steamer EGYPT, sunk on 20 May 1922 off Ushant after collision in fog with the steamer SEINE. The wreck was located in August 1930 by the salvage vessel ARTIGLIO which on 7 December was destroyed in an explosion whilst dispersing the wreck of FLORENCE H. A new ARTIGLIO recovered most of the bullion, value over £1 million, between 1931 and 1933 from a record depth of 360 feet. SORIMA developed the use of grabs controlled by a diver in an observation chamber.

In 1912-1913 three sisters were delivered, ANGLO-CALIFORNIAN, ANGLO-EGYPTIAN and ANGLO-BRAZILIAN. On dimensions of 425.0 x 56.3 x 36.3ft they averaged 7,400gt and were followed by the even larger ANGLO-CHILEAN of over 9,000gt (with slight alterations of tonnage openings this was later reduced to 7,137gt). The delivery of ANGLO-CALIFORNIAN was delayed from November 1911 to May 1912 by strikes in the shipyard. Rumour also suggested Latta had refused an offer for two of these new steamers which would have given a profit of £20,000 to £30,000 each.

Before the contract for ANGLO-CALIFORNIAN was placed, a careful study was undertaken of the new diesel engine powered tonnage which was in the news. Although the Danish SELANDIA is usually credited with being the first seagoing motorship, completed in 1912 with twin Burmeister and Wain diesels, Latta was referring to earlier and often overlooked vessels. For some years early diesels had been installed in tankers and cargo vessels for the Caspian Sea and Russian river trade, but in the summer of 1910 ROMAGNA (678gt) was completed in Italy with two Sulzer diesels, followed later in the year by the Dutch built tanker VULCANUS (1179gt) for the Royal Dutch/Shell Consortium. ROMAGNA had only a short life, she foundered off Rovigno on 24 November 1911, but VULCANUS lasted until broken up late in 1931, at which time her original engine, the first Werkspoor marine diesel, was recovered for further use.

---

**Position Report—30 May 1912**

ANGLO-AUSTRALIAN—arrived Bahia Blanca 11 May from Newport.
ANGLO-BOLIVIAN—arrived Newcastle NSW 29 May to load for Valparaiso.
ANGLO-CALIFORNIAN—arrived Narvik 27 May from the Tyne.
ANGLO-CANADIAN—sailed Coronel 18 May for Savannah.
ANGLO-COLOMBIAN—arrived Coronel 28 May from Taltal.
ANGLO-MEXICAN—arrived Norfolk (Va) 28 May from Philadelphia.
ANGLO-PATAGONIAN—arrived Charleston 27 May from Caleta Colosa.
ANGLO-SAXON—sailed New York 24 April and Sewall's Point 26 April for Auckland, passed Cape Henry 27 April.
SOUTH AMERICA—wrecked at St Loy 13 March.
SOUTH AUSTRALIA—sailed Port Talbot 26 May for Coronel.

---

The design of company ships was forward thinking, for instance all ships since 1900 had double riveted tanks for oil fuel, provision being made to burn both coal and oil. Latta was strongly in favour of keeping coal for British merchant and naval use in view of the abundant national resources, and the fear that an enemy might gain control of oil supplies during wartime. For Nitrate Producers' coal was plentiful, cheap and increasingly efficient. The company had an extensive trade in British, Chilean and New Zealand coal which was advantageous when compared to the limited availability of oil. The ANGLO boats were specially designed for the Chilean trade, with deep water ports in Europe and North America and limited depths in Chilean ports. They had bunkers which enabled them to sail from Europe with sufficient fuel on

ANGLO-EGYPTIAN discharging 2300 tons of machinery and construction material for the new Broken Hill Pty steelworks, Newcastle NSW, 20 December 1913
(BHP Archives/N1291)

board for the return trip, the fuel burnt on the outward passage meant they could load a maximum cargo in Chile without draught problems. This worked well and could not be improved on by a motorship, the first costs of which would considerably exceed those of a comparable steamer.

"Lloyd's Weekly Shipping Index" for 30 May 1912 gives a clear picture of the close association of the fleet with South America. Of the ten ships trading SOUTH AMERICA had just been lost, seven were in, or on passage for, American waters, two were trading to Australia and New Zealand, whilst ANGLO-CALIFORNIAN was in the Narvik iron ore trade.

# TITANIC AND CALIFORNIAN *6*

Probably the best known master in the fleet took over ANGLO-SAXON in March 1913. He was Stanley Lord, previously of the Leyland Line. Born at Bolton in 1877 he went to sea as an apprentice in 1891, on the iron barque NAIAD. After obtaining his second mate's ticket he made a voyage on the barque LURLEI. These early years at sea were mainly in the nitrate trade.

With a new first mate's ticket he moved into steam, taking a berth as third officer on the West India and Pacific Steam Navigation Company's BARBADIAN. When the Leyland Line purchased that company in 1900 he continued with the new owners who shortly became part of the International Mercantile Marine. Rising steadily Lord was mate of the ANTILLIAN when, in 1906, Captain Japha had to stay ashore due to illness. Taking temporary command of ANTILLIAN Lord was given his own ship, LOUISIANIAN, a year later. WILLIAM CLIFF followed and, in March 1911, CALIFORNIAN.

On passage from London for Boston CALIFORNIAN met extensive ice late on Sunday 14 April 1912. Being fitted with wireless she had previously passed ice warnings to TITANIC, on her maiden voyage. The operator on TITANIC had been rather peremptory with his opposite number on CALIFORNIAN, preferring to pass commercial traffic to the shore station. CALIFORNIAN therefore went off the air and it was not until dawn that news of the tragedy was received. TITANIC had hit an iceberg at speed and sunk with the loss of some 1,500 lives.

Immediately Lord worked his ship through the ice and made for the position given for the sinking of TITANIC. It took CALIFORNIAN from 6am to 8.30am at her full speed of about 13 knots to reach CARPATHIA which had just finished embarking survivors.

At the subsequent Court of Inquiry Captain Lord and others of his crew were called as witnesses. Lord found himself in a hostile court already biased by rumour and press account. With no opportunity to defend himself he found Lord Mersey's report condemned him as responsible for the loss of life. Lord Mersey, chairman of the Inquiry, refused to accept that CALIFORNIAN had been so far north of TITANIC as had been stated in evidence. A problem

*Captain Stanley Lord*

was several unidentified vessels were in the vicinity of both ships, probably not fitted with wireless which was still a novelty carried by few. Many years later one of these unidentified vessels was named as the illegal sealer SAMSON.

Many consider Lord to have been sacrificed as a scapegoat. The debate has continued ever since and because of it the Merchant Shipping Act, 1970, incorporates the right of appeal which Captain Lord did not possess and was repeatedly refused. A number of attempts to locate the wreck of the TITANIC failed until, on 1 September 1985, the expedition led by Dr Robert Ballard of the Woods Hole Oceanographic Institution, working from the research vessel KNORR, succeeded in discovering it and establishing a true position. Finally, the Secretary of State for Transport ordered a reappraisal of the role played by CALIFORNIAN, the findings of which were published in 1992.

The reappraisal highlighted the problems of reviewing events after a lapse of eighty years. Whilst there was disagreement on various points at the Marine Investigation Branch, the report concluded CALIFORNIAN was probably 18 miles from TITANIC and would not have been able to reach her in time to save more lives. This is consistent with both vessels using powerful morse lamps and yet not seeing the other. The reappraisal suggests Captain Lord's failure to respond to messages from the bridge were consistent with somnambulism. The report believes rockets fired from the TITANIC were seen, but the officer of the watch failed to read any urgency into what he saw. There was great ambiguity in the use of rockets in 1912, a situation that was not rectified for a further 35 years.

Returning to the Leyland Line Lord was horrified to discover they were not prepared to offer him further command. Although the Liverpool management supported him, and later provided full references, the board of directors in London gave way to one of their number, the influential Sir Miles Mattinson, who threatened resignation if Lord was given another ship.

At this stage John Latta and the Nitrate Producers' Steamship Company came into Stanley Lord's life. Having received a recommendation from an old friend, Frank Strachan whose company, the Strachan Shipping Company, were Leyland Line agents at Savannah, Georgia, Latta asked Captain Lord to visit him at the company offices in London. John Latta was fully aware of the circumstances surrounding Lord's departure from the Leyland Line and showed his opinion of Lord Mersey's "findings" and the accusations against him by offering Lord a command. Early in March 1913 Captain Lord was at sea again in command of ANGLO-SAXON, his salary being £20 a month plus a £5 monthly bonus. In the coming years Lord was to take all new ships to sea, in effect being commodore of the fleet. This fits John Latta's character as was later recorded by John Warr who worked as a footman in the Latta household about 1933, and later as butler with Bruce Ismay. His comment was "Sir John ... was very just and one could always talk to him about any grievances, and he would always listen to one's troubles."

Lord transferred from ANGLO-SAXON at short notice in 1914, to ANGLO-PATAGONIAN. His relief then was further delayed by the death of Captain Parslow in his defence of ANGLO-CALIFORNIAN. Sent north to Sunderland he then stood by the new ANGLO-CHILEAN and took her to sea, having a close shave in May 1917 when attacked by U38 (Korvettenkapitän Max Valentiner) which had just sunk the steamer RIO AMAZONAS. There was a two hour gun battle in which 67 shells were counted as fired by U38, in response to which ANGLO-CHILEAN fired seven rounds before she was able to escape.

Lord resigned from the company and retired from the sea on doctor's advice in July 1928. Sadly his fight to have his reputation restored was repeatedly rejected and when he died in January 1962 he still stood unjustly condemned by Lord Mersey's report.

The steady improvement in financial returns experienced in 1912-1913 were shattered by events in the summer of 1914. Although returns for shipowners in the next four years would be higher than ever before this had to be offset against horrendous loss of life and ships in the merchant marine as World War I took its course. In Sarajevo Gavrilo Princip, the student who fired the fatal shots on 28 June 1914 killing the heir to the Austro-Hungarian throne, Archduke Franz Ferdinand and his morganatic wife, Sophie the Archduchess of Hohenberg, could not have anticipated the dire consequences.

*ANGLO-BOLIVIAN*

On 4 August 1914 Britain declared war on Germany in defence of Belgian neutrality. For the duration there would be no risk of layups and poor markets, the demand for tonnage would exceed that available. The Anglo Line was to be in the forefront of the action and was in a position to benefit financially, the fleet which had cost £692,654 to build had been written down to £265,679 and reserves stood at £91,688. Latta had early in his career been influenced by companies who had issued shares only partly paid up, then paid high dividends and not built reserve funds. When the freight market fell they called up additional capital to fund the shortfall, and this often revealed some shareholders, widows and the like, unable to meet the call. He therefore firmly believed in retaining funds to ensure such calls were never made.

The fleet was widely scattered. Only ANGLO-CANADIAN was in European waters, loading at Cardiff for Valparaiso. Over half were engaged in trade between Chile and the United States. ANGLO-BOLIVIAN was at New Orleans and ANGLO-MEXICAN at Savannah, from where she sailed on 4 August for London. Further north ANGLO-BRAZILIAN was in the St Lawrence, having arrived from the Tyne in late July. Having sustained grounding damage in the river later in August she dry-docked at Montreal. Both ANGLO-COLOMBIAN and ANGLO-SAXON were on the Chilean coast loading at Mejillones and Pisagua respectively for the United States. ANGLO-PATAGONIAN and ANGLO-AUSTRALIAN were both at sea, the first in the Straits of Magellan on passage from Iquique for Charleston, whilst ANGLO-AUSTRALIAN had earlier sailed from Iquique but hit a rock and diverted leaking to Pernambuco. After repairs, she sailed for Philadelphia and Baltimore and was now east of Trinidad. Further afield ANGLO-CALIFORNIAN was off the Mexican coast on passage from Iquique for San Francisco, whilst ANGLO-EGYPTIAN was in the Indian Ocean, on passage from Montreal for Sydney via Natal.

The outbreak of war overshadowed the opening of the Panama Canal two weeks later. Conceived as long ago as the 16th century, it was Ferdinand de Lesseps, of Suez Canal fame, who commenced work in 1881 and made the first real attempt to realise the goal of joining the Pacific and Atlantic Oceans. The undertaking failed, going into liquidation in 1889, fever and malaria being the major causes. In 1902 the United States Government purchased the rights to the project and, after eradicating

*Mercantile Marine War Medal, 1914-1918.*

**Position Report—4 August 1914**

ANGLO-AUSTRALIAN—sailed Iquique 23 May. Hit rock in 09°04'S 35°10'W, diverted Pernambuco to repair, sailed 31 July for Philadelphia and Baltimore, arrived 7 September.
ANGLO-BOLIVIAN—at New Orleans, arrived 17 July from Iquique.
ANGLO-BRAZILIAN—sailed Shields 14 July, passed Fame Point 1 August, arrived Montreal 25 August.
ANGLO-CALIFORNIAN—sailed Iquique 25 July, arrived San Francisco 9 August.
ANGLO-CANADIAN—arrived Cardiff 27 July, loading for Valparaiso.
ANGLO-COLOMBIAN—on West Coast. Arrived Mollendo 17 July from Cardiff. Sailed Mejillones 31 August for Charleston.
ANGLO-EGYPTIAN—sailed Montreal 20 June and Natal 23 July for Sydney, arrived 20 August.
ANGLO-MEXICAN—sailed Savannah 4 August for London, arrived 21 August.
ANGLO-PATAGONIAN—sailed Iquique 29 July for Charleston, arrived 18 September.
ANGLO-SAXON—on West Coast. Arrived Valparaiso 25 June from Blyth. Sailed Pisagua 27 August for Savannah.

(Lloyd's Weekly Index)

the cause of disease, proceeded to realise the dream. Although it was 1920 before President Wilson declared the canal formally open, commercial use of the passage had commenced on 15 August 1914.

The first British transit was of the Glasgow owned DALDORCH, the 14th commercial transit, on 22 August. On passage from Tacoma for Limerick with a cargo of wheat she had sailed on 4 August and been instructed by radio to divert when off Cape San Lucia. It was estimated she saved 40 days on her intended passage via the Straits of Magellan. The canal shortened the passage from North Pacific ports, such as Vancouver and San Francisco, to Liverpool by over 5,600 miles or 24 days' steaming at 10 knots. From Iquique to Liverpool over 2,300 miles was saved (10 days at 10 knots), and from Iquique to New York 4,500 miles (19 days).

Latta had all along recognised the value of the canal for his trade between Europe, North America and the West Coast of South America. Hence ANGLO-SAXON was the 3rd British ship to transit, the 28th commercial, when she passed northwards on 6 September, followed by ANGLO-COLOMBIAN (6th British: 36th commercial) on 11 September and ANGLO-CALIFORNIAN (7th British: 41st commercial) on 16 September.

The outbreak of war found Arthur Westacott in command of ANGLO-COLOMBIAN, and Frederick Richardson had ANGLO-BRAZILIAN. A West Countryman from Barnstaple, Westacott had joined the SOUTH AMERICA as mate in July 1908 and taken command in November 1909. He spent the rest of his seagoing career with the company, ending in 1926, at the age of 51 when he came ashore from the second ANGLO-COLOMBIAN. A Welshman born at Cardiff in 1866, Richardson's first command had been the steamer MONTANA in 1900. Taking Latta's ANGLO-CHILIAN in May 1911 he commanded four other Anglo boats before tendering his resignation and leaving ANGLO-PATAGONIAN in February 1916. Like Lewis and Isaacs before him he moved to Court Line, taking CRESSINGTON COURT in May 1916. When she was sold to the Sutherland Steamship Company Ltd (managed by B.J. Sutherland and Company Ltd, Newcastle) in August 1918, and renamed

ROXBURGH in November 1919, he remained with her until his death, which took place on 10 December 1919.

ANGLO-CANADIAN never finished loading for Valparaiso, being taken over for Government service on 6 August as a cross Channel supply ship for the British forces in France. Government service continued until her sinking in January 1918. ANGLO-EGYPTIAN, commanded by Captain Greenhill, was also taken over, in Australia by the Australian Government on 7 September to become Transport A25. The despatch of colonial troops from Australia and New Zealand was delayed due to uncertainty over the whereabouts of units of the German Pacific Fleet which included the armoured cruisers SCHARNHORST and GNEISENAU (both subsequently sunk at the Battle of the Falkland Islands on 8 December). The consequences should such enemy ships find and attack an inadequately protected troop convoy were too horrendous to consider. However, as sufficient Allied warships became available the loaded transports started to converge late in October, coming together off Albany in King George Sound. ANGLO-EGYPTIAN had loaded at Brisbane and Melbourne before sailing for King George Sound with 12 officers, 100 men and 549 horses. On 1 November this first Anzac troop convoy sailed, the transports A1-28 and NZ3-12 escorted by the armoured cruiser MINOTAUR, the Japanese battle cruiser IBUKI and the two scout cruisers MELBOURNE and SYDNEY. Routed via Colombo, Aden and through the

---

**War Service—1914 to 1918**

ANGLO-CANADIAN
    6.8.1914-28.11.1916 Expeditionary Force transport 180 cross-Channel.
    29.11.1916-18.4.1917 USA to UK, wheat & horses.
    20.4.1917-27.5.1917 collier transport 1572.
    28.5.1917-24.8.1917 USA to UK, wheat & horses.
    25.8.1917-22.1.1918 transport B8126, USA to Egypt, horses.
                    Mediterranean trooping.
    22.1.1918 torpedoed and sunk.
ANGLO-EGYPTIAN
    7.9.1914-16.4.1917 Australian transport A25.
    (15.3.1915-20.3.1916 Imperial service)
    17.4.1917-4.10.1917 transport F0286. Natives West to East Africa.
    5.10.1917-16.10.1918 Australia to India, horses. Troops & remounts to Mediterranean.
    17.10.1918-7.11.1918 French Government service.
    8.11.1918-mid 1919 Expeditionary Force service.
ANGLO-SAXON
    22.11.1915-12.12.1915 Expeditionary Force transport.
    5.10.1918-mid 1919 collier transport 2375.
ANGLO-CHILEAN
    28.3.1917-26.5.1917 Expeditionary Force transport, London to Alexandria.
    27.5.1917-14.8.1917 wheat from USA.
    15.8.1917-7.10.1917 collier transport 1726.
    8.10.1917-17.12.1917 Expeditionary Force transport, hay & oats.
    18.12.1917-26.6.1918 Expeditionary Force transport C086.
                    Wheat & horses from USA and Canada.
    27.6.1918-8.9.1918 wheat from USA.
    9.9.1918-10.4.1919 collier transport 1726.
ANGLO-MEXICAN
    30.8.1918-9.11.1918 US Government service. Stores USA to France.
    10.11.1918-mid 1919 collier transport 2416.

---

Suez Canal, the danger from enemy ships was highlighted when, nearing the Cocos Islands, SYDNEY was detached to catch and destroy the German light cruiser EMDEN on 9 November. ANGLO-EGYPTIAN survived the war, although chased by a submarine on 16 April 1917 in the Mediterranean when her speed enabled her to escape. ANGLO-CHILEAN was requisitioned new in 1917, despite John Latta's protests that new ships were normally allowed one voyage on the open market before being pressed into service. ANGLO-SAXON and ANGLO-MEXICAN served for shorter periods.

*ANGLO-CHILEAN.*  *(World Ship Photo Library)*

The oldest ship in the fleet, ANGLO-AUSTRALIAN, was sold in 1915 for £68,750: the war was already showing its influence as this price compares with her new cost of £47,000. The buyers were B.J. Sutherland and Company Ltd, Newcastle, who immediately resold her to London owners for £73,000. Renamed CALONNE she was to carry the names BYZANTION, EKATERINA INGLESSI and EKATERINA C before dragging her anchors and driving ashore in the River Plate on 28 May 1927. A year later, underwriters having agreed a total loss, she was refloated and towed into Buenos Aires. Six months later she left for Genoa where she was broken up.

ANGLO-CALIFORNIAN, under the command of Captain Frederick Parslow, now Commodore of the fleet, was 90 miles south of Queenstown with horses from Montreal when she sighted U39 (Kapitänleutnant Forstmann) a mile off at 8am on 4 July 1915. U39 had been cruising in the area since 28 June and had already sunk twelve ships. Unbeknown to Captain Parslow who made every effort to stop U39 getting into a position to fire a torpedo, she had none left, hence surfacing to use her gun. Being unarmed Captain Parslow's choice was surrender or run for it. He chose the latter and a four hour chase developed with U39 closing and shelling. Captain Parslow then decided to surrender in view of the damage being taken and to save life, but receiving a radio signal that the destroyers MENTOR and MIRANDA were on their way he called the men back from the boats and got under way again to continue avoiding action. U39 was now close to ANGLO-CALIFORNIAN and opened a heavy fire from the gun, machine guns and rifles on the deck and bridge where Captain Parslow continued to command with his son, the second mate, at the wheel. Twenty one lives were lost in the shelling, including Captain Parslow killed on the bridge by a bursting shell, believed to be the last left for the submarine gun.

This was the second loss sustained by the family, for on 8 May 1915 his second son Frank Parslow, a rifleman with the London Regiment, had been killed at Ypres whilst serving in the Machine Gun Corps. The action of Captain Parslow was recognised by a posthumous Victoria Cross, his son and the Chief Engineer, James Crawford, both receiving the Distinguished Service Cross. The Admiralty and Lloyd's of London made monetary and other awards to the crew and Lloyd's Silver Medal for Meritorious Services was conferred on Captain Parslow. Amongst the awards were inscribed gold watches from the Admiralty to the Chief Officer, Harold Read, for his gallantry and to the young chief radio officer, John Rea, who remained operating the radio throughout the action, at times lying flat on the floor with shrapnel cutting through the cabin. John Rea went on to be torpedoed twice in the war, when TARQUAH was sunk on 7 December 1917 and AUSONIA on 30 May 1918. Between the wars he served mainly on Elder Dempster Line ships and had

Captain Frederick Parslow, VC.

U39 attacking ANGLO-CALIFORNIAN, sketched by Charles Bryant for the Sydney Mail. (Redrawn by D. Gowing)

Lloyd's Silver Medal for Meritorious Service.

Kapitänleutnant Walter Forstmann.

# The VICTORIA CROSS

A military decoration, only two have been awarded to Merchant Navy personnel, both announced in the London Gazette for 24 May 1919. In both cases the recipients were posthumously commissioned as Lieutenants RNR, to make them eligible.

In addition to Frederick Parslow and ANGLO-CALIFORNIAN, the award was bestowed on Archibald Smith of the New Zealand Shipping Company's OTAKI. Sighted by the German raider MÖWE on 10 March 1917, she refused to surrender and defended herself with a single 4.7 inch gun against MÖWE's four 15cm and smaller. Captain Smith was lost with his ship which was sunk in the action, leaving the raider damaged and on fire. It took three days to extinguish the blaze.

APAPA bombed and sunk under him on 15 November 1940. He finally retired from the sea in 1959.

As will be mentioned later, ANGLO-CALIFORNIAN was not to survive the war. But U39 did, and surrendered to France where she was broken up in 1923. One of a class of eleven submarines, U31-U41, completed in 1914-1915, three others also survived, U33 and U35 allocated to Britain and U38 which went to France. The fates of the others gives a picture of the risks faced by submarines in wartime. U31 disappeared, probably sunk by a mine, in January 1915, followed by U37, victim of a mine on 1 April 1915. Several were to fall to Q-ships, innocent looking merchant vessels converted into heavily armed warships trailing their coat tails inviting attack. U40 was an early victim, torpedoed by the British submarine C24 off Aberdeen on 24 June 1915. C24 was partnered by the trawler TARANAKI (A445) which acted both as bait and was also armed. U40 engaged in a gun action with TARANAKI, unaware that C24 was stalking her. A month later U36 fell victim to the Q-ship PRINCE CHARLES off the Hebrides, and on 24 September 1915 U41 was caught by the Q-ship WYANDRA off the Scillies. WYANDRA is better known as BARALONG, having sunk U27 on 19 August 1915. In the action survivors from the U-boat crew had been hunted down and killed, leading to the cry of atrocity. This German reply to British charges of submarine outrages was responsible for delaying the entry of the United States into the conflict. Sinkings did not go all one way, U38 was credited with despatching two Q-ships, REMEMBRANCE in the Mediterranean on 14 August 1916 and WARNER off the Irish coast on 13 March 1917. Finally two more of the submarines were lost to Allied naval action before the Armistice, U32 a victim of the Flower class sloop WALLFLOWER in the Mediterranean on 8 May 1918 and, only days from the return of peace, U34 sunk by the Q-ship PRIVET off Gibraltar.

John Latta was an outspoken critic of the methods employed by the Admiralty when chartering ships for Government service and paying "Blue Book" rates of hire. Different rates were paid for liner and tramp tonnage, the classification of which was paid had nothing to do with the ships concerned, but was based on an arbitrary classification of the owners. The Nitrate Producers' Steamship Company held a privileged position in Chile, where by ukase of the Government they enjoyed all the privileges of liners. But in England although they were of the highest class of cargo liner and of exceptional value to the war effort, ideally suited for employment as troopships, they were classified in "Blue Book" rates alongside the cheapest tramp. Appeals to the Admiralty finally brought some response in March 1917, the difference between liner and tramp tonnage was divided and Lawther, Latta and Company received a hire rate increase of 1s 6d. However, by this time Latta had sold three of the ships to liner companies and with the change of ownership their charter rates immediately moved to the liner scale. Union-Castle took ANGLO-BRAZILIAN for £200,000 and renamed her CHEPSTOW CASTLE. Her value in liner trade was obvious when they retained her after the war, until she went to the breakers in 1932. Cunard took the other two, ANGLO-CALIFORNIAN, repaired after her fight with U39, for £215,000. Renamed VANDALIA, she nearly survived the war, being torpedoed and sunk by U96 on 9 June 1918. They also took ANGLO-BOLIVIAN for £190,000, and she became VINOVIA until torpedoed by U105 on 19 December 1917. In 1953 Risdon Beazley's salvage vessel HELP located the wreck of VINOVIA in 200 feet of water and later returned to recover 694 tons of copper and zinc from her cargo, mainly in 1957.

The fleet was to lose three ships to enemy action. The first was ANGLO-COLUMBIAN, sunk by gunfire from Kapitänleutnant Hansen's U41 on 23 September 1915. Sailing from Wilhelmshaven, U41's first success was ANGLO-COLUMBIAN, followed by CHANCELLOR and HESIONE. She then attacked URBINO the following day (24 September), only to be surprised and sunk by the Q-ship BARALONG. There were only two survivors, Oberleutnant Crompton and helmsman Godau, who spent two hours in the water and on one of URBINO's abandoned lifeboats before being taken on board BARALONG. Their treatment there and after landing, especially the lack of proper care for Crompton's head wound, threatened to feature the BARALONG in the international press for a second time. The first had been when BARALONG (Lieutenant Commander Godfrey Herbert) sank U27 on 19 August 1915, all the submarine crew being massacred. This "Baralong incident" reverberated through the politics of the time, giving a German reply to accusations of submarine atrocities and helped dissuade President Woodrow Wilson from bringing America into the war at that stage of the conflict.

ANGLO-PATAGONIAN was the next loss on 10 July 1917 as has been mentioned, and she was followed by ANGLO-CANADIAN sunk by the Austrian KuK U27 (Linienschiffsleutnant Josef Holub) on 22 January 1918. Employed as a troopship, she was on passage from Alexandria for Marseilles in ballast, but with 46 British and 167 officers and men of the Indian Labour Corps on board. In a seven knot convoy of 16 ships, she was lost at the same time as MANCHESTER SPINNER. Some sources claim the German U63 was responsible but research indicates the Austrian as being the victor. U63 sank the Italian steamer ANDREA COSTA from the convoy and this has been confused with ANGLO-CANADIAN. The first torpedo hit the port side of number two hold at 3.18pm and an hour later, as the ship was being abandoned, a second torpedo hit the engine room and she went down three minutes later. Brigadier General J.B. Pollock-McCall, in command of the troops, reported "The Ship's crew behaved in the most exemplary way, and arrangements of Captain Splatt and Chief Officer Bertram Day were perfect." Both Captain Splatt and Chief Officer Day were commended in the "London Gazette" of 7 June 1918, along with Lieutenant Pierce of the Royal Welsh Fusiliers and Second Lieutenant Cooper of the Essex Regiment. Although holding command since 1890 Captain Splatt had only joined Nitrate Producers' in 1913, taking ANGLO-CANADIAN until her loss. He was next sent to ANGLO-EGYPTIAN and was her master from 1918 to 1927. Early the following year he took ANGLO-INDIAN to sea for a few months until retiring on 8 September 1928. He died on 15 November 1933. Day was afterwards sent to ANGLO-CHILEAN as mate, taking command in 1926 and remained with the company to the end, signing off ANGLO-INDIAN in February 1943.

The outbreak of war in 1914 found Short Brothers' yard number 390 under construction for delivery in August 1915. Along with all other civilian orders work on her ceased on Admiralty instructions to concentrate on Government war contracts. In due course hulls occupying berths required for Admiralty work were completed and launched to make them available and then work restarted as labour and materials became available and the need for merchant ships grew to fill the yawning gaps left by submarine sinkings. ANGLO-CHILEAN, as number 390 became, was finally launched on 2 May 1916 and completed in November 1916 ready for Captain Lord to take on trials. She limped back to the shipyard from trials with her low pressure cylinder cracked and remained there another four months whilst repairs were completed. From this developed a law case which was finally settled by the House of Lords in 1921. Latta would have settled for £20,000, the engine builders offered

£15,000 and the final award in 1921 was £50,000.

The correspondence between John Latta and his brother-in-law, Thomas Short, throws an interesting light on the question of marine engineering and quadruple expansion. Due to the wartime situation the engines for ANGLO-CHILEAN came from George Clark Ltd, Sunderland, whereas for years the suppliers had been North Eastern Marine. It was felt the crack had been caused by the casting being taken from the sand mould too quickly, a practice that North Eastern Marine avoided. The correspondence reviewed the history of quadruple expansion and the early attempts by William Allan and Company and James Knott's Prince Line to perfect the four stage expansion. Allan had built an example for ARABIAN PRINCE in 1889, which was tripled in 1900.

The Scotia Engine Works erected seven such engines. One went into the first ship to load frozen meat from the River Plate in 1883, MEATH owned by R.M. Hudson, Sunderland, and on charter to Houlder Brothers. Lengthened and re-engined in 1889 (she had been built in 1879 with compound machinery), she was converted to triple in 1897. Tripling of Allan's quads was relatively simple as the high and first intermediate pressure cylinders were mounted athwartship and drove through a single crosshead to a common crank.

Four of the engines were the same size, ARABIAN PRINCE, REGINA, ENCHANTRESS and PARAHYBA. Five were altered to triples in 1897/1900, three by Allan and one each by Clark and North Eastern Marine. Of the other two, SOMERTON was wrecked in 1896 and only PARAHYBA retained her original engine to the end, torpedoed in 1917. Four of the sets were fitted in hulls built by Short Brothers, hence the familiarity of Short and Latta with the problems. Osbourne, Graham and Company, and William Doxford and Sons each took one set.

During and after the war Lawther, Latta and Company were appointed managers of six ships on behalf of the Admiralty and the Shipping Controller. The first, for a brief period in 1914/1915, was HUNSGATE. Completed in 1911 as the German ALTAIR she had been captured in the Red Sea by HMS DUKE OF EDINBURGH soon after the outbreak of war and as a prize had been taken over by the Admiralty and renamed HUNSGATE. Transferred to the management of William Robertson, Glasgow, in 1915 she was sold after the war to become GURTH and MOGHREB ACSA. Wrecked near Honfleur on 14 July 1928 she broke in two and navigation had to be temporarily suspended due to the risk of damage to propellers from the wine casks which floated free.

To offset the submarine sinkings, especially after unrestricted sinkings commenced in February 1917, a special shipbuilding programme of standard designs was commenced. These ships were placed under the ownership of the Shipping Controller who arranged for management by various shipping companies. William Gray and Company at West Hartlepool received orders for two E-type ships, both of which were assigned to Lawther, Latta and Company to manage. The first of these was launched on 25 July 1918 as WAR WAGTAIL. Sold to Cunard in 1919 and renamed VINDELIA she passed to Indian owners in 1924 as JALAJYOTI and was broken up at Bombay in 1950.

Her sister never reached Lawther Latta's hands. Intended to be named WAR REDTAIL she was launched in June 1919 and sold before completion. Entering service as HOMAYUN, she later became the Greek AGHIOS MARKOS and was bombed by German aircraft off Salamis Island on 22 April 1941.

Under the terms of the Peace Agreement the vast majority of ships in the German Mercantile Marine were surrendered to the Allied Shipping Commission and allocated amongst the Allied countries. Three of those transferred to Britain were, in 1919, placed under the management of Lawther, Latta and Company, BERMUDA, ERFURT and FÜRST BÜLOW. The oldest was BERMUDA, dating from 1899 when completed as SAINT ANDREW. Sold to Indian owners in 1921 as ENGLESTAN she was broken up in 1932 as the Italian MARIA ADELE. FÜRST BÜLOW was built in 1911 for the Hamburg America Line and was sold back to them in 1921, whilst ERFURT was a wartime completion intended for Norddeutscher Lloyd which in 1922 became the Belgian MERCIER and was torpedoed off Newfoundland by U204 on 9 June 1941.

During the war some 28 of the seagoing staff had been killed by enemy action, a relatively small price when compared with other fleets. The only good that had come from the war was that shipowners, for a change, had good bank balances, although if all owners had replaced their lost tonnage at current prices the insurance payments received from the Government would not have come anywhere near meeting the cost. Rather than blindly rebuild, most owners chose to wait and review the market situation before deciding their course of action and John Latta did just so. Apart from the purchase of one ex-German ship he waited until 1925 before commissioning new tonnage. The purchase was the big Hansa ship SCHWARZENFELS in 1921. Renamed ANGLO-COLOMBIAN she was retained until 1936, when sold back to German owners and renamed AFRIKA. The same year, on 21 December, she foundered north of Trondheim bound from Narvik with a cargo of iron ore for Emden.

In the closing days of the war ANGLO-CHILEAN was leader of a convoy from New York to the United Kingdom, carrying Captain W.H. Owen, RNR as Convoy Commodore. For twenty years a Marine Superintendent in the West Indies for the Royal Mail Steam Packet Company, Captain Owen complemented John Latta on his "splendidly equipped ship" and the "loyal and able man in command", Captain Lord. He also praised the practical assistance of Third Officer Johnson and apprentice Goodchild.

# RECESSION AND DEPRESSION *8*

With assets exceeding capital most companies chose to increase their capital to match and distributed paid up shares on a pro-rata basis. John Latta chose an entirely different, and possibly unique, method. He proposed to wind up the Nitrate Producers' Steamship Company Ltd and form a new company of the same name. His plan was to exchange the Preference shares for 5% War Bonds at par and to pay £40 in 5% War Loan for each £5 ordinary share. Alternatively shareholders could take £35 of Loans or Bonds for each ordinary share plus a paid up £5 share in the new company. The ships, goodwill, reserves and cash balance left would be transferred to the new company. By September 1918 only 90 of the 31,253 issued shares, held by two shareholders, had yet to reply and they soon after responded in line with all others accepting the offer and taking a holding in the new company. The only problem arose when the Inland Revenue objected. Past financial performance, prior to and during the war, was being taken into consideration in estimating tax liability and they were reluctant to see a new company which they might not be able to assess on that basis. It was agreed the new company should be taxed as if it were the old company and the objection was withdrawn. An extraordinary general meeting on 17 September 1918 agreed the voluntary liquidation of the old company and the new Nitrate Producers' Steamship Company Ltd was registered on 5 October 1918.

The first balance sheet for the new company was prepared on 30 April 1919, and covered the first six months trading. Whilst slight differences in layout make it difficult to compare with the April 1918 balance sheet of the old company, the healthy state of the accounts is clear. In April 1918 a total of £1,179,240 stood in the Reserve and Building Funds, a year later the Reserve Fund still stood at £409,450. Even after distributing £1,375,000 to retire the debenture bonds and pay £35 per ordinary share the new company commenced business with transferred reserves of £18 per share. The fleet of four steamers stood in the accounts at £5 10s 1d per ton deadweight, or less than a fourth of their market value. The cost of new tonnage was such that had, at that time, a vessel similar to ANGLO-CHILEAN been ordered practically all of the Reserve Fund would have been absorbed. But no such action was contemplated as John Latta's views (see below) on the likely post-war trend in business was soon to be vindicated. The full employment of the fleet during the war, despite the level of the "Blue Book" time charter rates, resulted in healthy balance sheets, despite the effect of the Excess Profits Duty imposed in 1915. Originally 50%, increased to 80% in 1917, it was levied on profits above the average of the last three years before the war. Fortunately for shipowners those had been prosperous years.

## Simplified Balance Sheets, 30 April 1918 and 30 April 1919
(the last one issued by the old company, and the first by the new company)

| | 1918 | 1919 |
|---|---|---|
| To Issued Capital— | | |
| Ordinary shares of £5 each | £156,265 | £156,300 |
| 5% Cumulative preference shares of £5 each | 110,000 | — |
| To Sundry creditors and bills payable | 50,914 | 61,972 |
| ,, Pending voyages — receipts in excess of disbursements and estimated profits | 116,438 | 30,943 |
| ,, Insurance Fund | 98,442 | 98,441 |
| ,, General Reserve Fund | 479,240 | — |
| ,, Deferred Building Fund | 700,000 | — |
| ,, Capital Reserve Account* | — | 409,450 |
| ,, Provision for excess profits and income taxes | 100,000 | 65,000 |
| ,, Profit and loss account | 37,266 | 31,908 |
| | £1,848,565 | £854,014 |

| | 1918 | 1919 |
|---|---|---|
| By Steamship Account — | | |
| Book value of steamers | £1,640,699† | £219,077 |
| investments | | 555,124 |
| ,, Unexpired insurances | 23,516 | 26,032 |
| ,, Sundry debtors and agents | 48,058 | 6,780 |
| ,, Cash at bankers | 136,292 | 47,001 |
| | £1,848,565 | £854,014 |

John Latta,
Robert A. Lawther, } Directors
James A. Walker, Secretary

*Capital reserve account — representing surplus of assets over liabilities as at the date of incorporation of the new company, and the amount by which the steamers are valued in excess of the book value as taken over from the old company.

The 1919 accounts are for a 6 month period only.

†The book value of steamers is the original cost less 4% p.a. depreciation (estimated 1918 book value £228,205).

John Latta had devoted his knowledge and experience to the Ministry of Shipping during the war, for which he was created a baronet in 1920, whilst his brother Andrew was appointed a KBE the following year for voluntary services during and after the war as Assistant Director of the Ship Management Branch at the Ministry of Shipping, in the management of requisitioned and ex-enemy ships. Following the reorganisation of Nitrate Producers' Steamship Company, in 1921 the partnership of Lawther, Latta and Company was turned into a limited liability company, Lawther, Latta and Company Ltd.

At the Annual General Meeting in June 1916 John Latta had stated "… immediately peace was declared rates must have an unexpected slump." He applied this belief in practical terms and maintained the prosperous record by refusing to order new ships at the inflated war and immediate post-war levels. Even after distributing some of the profits the new company continued to be an exceptionally prosperous concern. The prophesy on freight rates was fulfilled when the freight market collapsed in the summer of 1920, and with it many optimists who considered the good times would continue. An increasing number of ships were unemployed, and the Nitrate Producers' fleet spent much of the summer of 1921 laid up —

ANGLO-CHILEAN—in the Tyne from 4 January to 25 October.

ANGLO-EGYPTIAN—at Hull from 8 April to 14 August.

ANGLO-MEXICAN—at Newport from 17 January to 30 September.

ANGLO-SAXON—at Hull from 5 March to 13 August.

In the decade of recession that followed many companies went into liquidation, leaving others such as Nitrate Producers', managed on very conservative lines, to survive. Typical of those that collapsed was the Cardiff based Western Counties Shipping Company Ltd. Founded in July 1915 and managed by Edgar Edwards and Sons Ltd, its meteoric growth based on optimism and heavy borrowing was followed by an equally fast collapse as ship values plummeted. By 1920 the original capital of £30,000 had been increased to £3.3 million, including £800,000 of 6.5% debentures. In 1919 Walter Runciman and Company's Moor Line fleet was purchased for £1.8 million, followed in 1920 by the B.J. Sutherland and Company fleet for another £1.8 million. Early in 1920 the fleet was valued at nearly £4.4 million and profits of £1 million a year were forecast. The rapid collapse of ship values and the freight market saw a receiver appointed in 1921 on behalf of the debenture holders. B.J. Sutherland repossessed the ships purchased in 1920 in accordance with the terms of the sale, and the subsequent sale of the Western Counties fleet realised £976,150. In the end analysis, 78% of the funds invested in this overcapitalised and highly geared venture were lost.

The nitrate trade was also entering a troubled period, although the threat of artificial nitrates was alleviated by growing demand. But the markets were now different. In 1920 European and North American contracts for Chilean nitrate totalled 2.75 million tons, but only 1.45 million tons of this had been sold on. The situation for Chile was serious, as 75% of revenue came from the nitrate export tax. Germany had taken 800,000 tons a year prior to 1914, in 1922 she imported 25% of that tonnage. At the end of the 19th century Chile had supplied about 70% of the world needs for nitrogen fertiliser. In 1902 1.3 million tons was exported, rising to 2.8 million tons in 1913.

Various attempts to synthesise and fix nitrogen had been made, but none proved commercially viable until in 1909 Fritz Haber developed a process whereby nitrogen in the air was combined with hydrogen to produce ammonia. Developed further as the Haber-Bosch process it enabled a wide range of nitrogen compounds to be synthesised. The outbreak of war in 1914 and the cessation of supplies of nitrate from Chile, coupled with the demand for munitions from the military, led to a massive increase in the German capacity to produce the synthetic material which accounted for this reduced post-war trade. The process was also adopted in other countries and saw Chilean exports drop to a mere 433,000 tons in 1933. Since then it has grown again, to over 1 million tons after World War II, but the percentage share of the market is now minimal at about 1-2%.

Sir John Latta was able, with a fleet built mainly at pre-war prices, to contain the economic and shipping situation, although he was not helped by the tax bill. In 1921 tax reserves were £130,000 and the sum finally paid was £191,000 or 120% of the capital of the company. Operating expenses for the ships in 1920 were five times the pre-war figure, which should be considered when examining the table of earnings per ton deadweight on page 32. Cardiff bunker coal alone cost £4 a ton compared with 6s $7\frac{1}{2}$d. Strikes were an increasing problem: in June 1923 ANGLO-SAXON was undergoing survey on the Tyne when held up by a boilermakers' stoppage. Port delays were another growing problem. ANGLO-CHILEAN in January 1923 was at Hull when chartered to load home from Bombay. To position her it was decided to take a coal cargo out, but it would have taken three weeks to load at Cardiff so Latta sent her to Durban where a full cargo was lifted in just over three days. It proved more profitable, and quicker, to send her nearly 4,500 miles further than direct through Suez. Three more ships followed this pattern. The following year ANGLO-CHILEAN was held up for a month in the United Kingdom by strike action and lost three good charters. Some years later ANGLO-EGYPTIAN discharged 6,000 tons of ore at Middlesbrough in 12 days, with disbursements of £1,600. ANGLO-CHILEAN landed a similar cargo of 8,000 tons at Antwerp in 9 days at a cost of £696!

The changing pattern of employment is evident from "Lloyd's Daily Index" for 25 May 1922 —

---

**Position Report—25 May 1922**

ANGLO-CHILEAN—arrived Bombay 22 May from Karachi.
ANGLO-COLOMBIAN—sailed Sydney 1 April for Cardiff, sailed Las Palmas 22 May.
ANGLO-EGYPTIAN—sailed Sydney 20 April for London, sailed Port Natal 20 May.
ANGLO-MEXICAN—arrived Hong Kong 13 May from Manati.
ANGLO-SAXON— sailed Port Natal 17 May and Table Bay 23 May for Buenos Ayres.

---

Gamble North, an original director and younger brother of Colonel North, died in 1922. With an ageing fleet, the youngest nearly ten years old, Latta embarked on a rolling fleet replacement programme that would see six near sisters commissioned between 1925 and 1929. There would be slight differences

*ANGLO-COLOMBIAN (2) in Queen Alexandra Dock, Cardiff, October 1925.*

between ships as modern technology was explored, the two most obvious being monitor hull construction and diesel machinery. Tonnages would range from 5,268 to 5,601 gross and common dimensions would be around 426.0 x 58.0 x 26.0ft (440ft overall). The steamers would have quadruple expansion engines from North Eastern Marine with three boilers working at 220 lb/sq in, giving 2,100ihp and a speed of 10.5 knots.

Having closely watched the development of the motorship Sir John Latta was not yet ready to order one for Nitrate Producers', and it was to be late in 1927 before this step was taken. Earlier, in a letter to "The Times" published on 15 May 1925, his caution was apparent. He wrote —

"The diesel engine and the use of oil have given Continental shipowners an incentive, and in some ways an advantage, in world's transport competition which they did not possess when substantially dependent on Welsh coal. This, in a measure, may account for the enormous increase of tonnage built in that quarter. It does not, however, prove that Diesel ships, cost for cost, with oil at to-day's price, can carry goods more economically than steamers—which is what matters.

There are still great potentialities in coal, and, in view of its importance to the people of these islands, as well as to shipowners themselves, the latter should not be too much influenced by what Continental shipowners and engineers are doing. I am not of the opinion that it has been clearly demonstrated that motor-vessels can transport goods under to-day's conditions more economically than steamers."

First to be launched on 7 July 1925 was ANGLO-INDIAN which had the Millar system of corrugated sides under the Monitor patent. These gave a wider beam of 59.5ft and carried a claim of extra cargo capacity, strength and better speed and fuel economy. ANGLO-PERUVIAN was completed in July 1926 and ANGLO-AUSTRALIAN followed, launched on 21 March 1927. ANGLO-CANADIAN, completed in July 1928, was the vessel chosen to be the trial motorship, being fitted with a locally designed and built four cylinder Doxford opposed-piston unit of 2,400bhp. At a price of £130,000 she cost £35,000 more than each of the two steamers which followed, a distinct disadvantage in the economic climate of the period. ANGLO-SAXON and ANGLO-AFRICAN, both completed in 1929, were the remaining units of the series. They were steamers like ANGLO-PERUVIAN and ANGLO-AUSTRALIAN. To build ANGLO-SAXON and ANGLO-AFRICAN a Trade Facility Act guarantee for £180,000 was obtained from the Treasury, although unlike some companies Nitrate Producers' repaid the loan obtained under the guarantee on schedule over the next six years.

ANGLO-INDIAN was placed in general trading, and in July 1926 arrived at Barrow with 9,000 tons of American coal to alleviate the shortage caused by the General Strike called for 4 May 1926. Although the General Strike only lasted nine days the miners continued their action for nearly six months, until November.

In discussing Latta's new ships the magazine "Shipbuilding and Shipping Record" commented on the past and present fleet in the issue of 2 June 1927 —

59

ANGLO-INDIAN (1). *(World Ship Photo Library)*

"At one time the Nitrate Producers' Steamship Company was mainly identified with the industry from which it takes its name, and the practise of the management was always to build a particularly fine type of cargo vessel. It was really of an intermediate liner type, and when all shipping was requisitioned during the war, it became a question of the rates of hire to which this tonnage was fairly entitled. Since the nitrate industry has long been depressed the company has, in recent years, sought other employment for some of its ships. At the annual meeting the other day, Sir John Latta, the chairman, stated that three of the vessels had been relegated to ordinary cargo trades, "where they cannot compete on level terms with less costly and more economical tonnage." The company has, in consequence, been experimenting with ships of lower power, designed to carry goods at a minimum cost. To this purpose it has built three steamers of 10,000 tons capacity, but each differing slightly in design. They give, Sir John Latta announced, "an unmistakable 10 knots" on 28 tons daily consumption of coal, and he knows of no more economical ships. A fourth vessel, fitted with Diesel machinery, is to be built, which will at first hand enable the management to test the internal-combustion engine with the most economical steam engine. The management, and Sir John Latta in particular, have always given the closest attention to the design of the ships of the fleet and their machinery, and the decision to build a motor vessel is another point in favour of this type. At the same time the company is taking no undue risks. We have no doubt that the management have been watching very carefully the experience with existing motor vessels."

As planned, to test of the diesel powered ship, it was arranged for her to undertake an identical voyage to one of the steamers to provide comparative data. ANGLO-AUSTRALIAN was the steamer chosen and the two voyages were —

ANGLO-AUSTRALIAN

Sailed Shields 16 December 1927; passed Table Bay 13 January 1928; at Port Pirie 4 February to 6 March 1928; at Durban 29 to 31 March 1928; passed Table Bay 3 April 1928; arrived Avonmouth 27 April 1928.

ANGLO-CANADIAN

Sailed Shields 5 August 1928; passed Table Bay 30 August 1928; at Port Pirie 21 September to 16 October 1928; passed Table Bay 2 November 1928; arrived Avonmouth 8 December 1928.

Sir John Latta noted the efficiency and general adaptability of the Doxford diesel, time was saved by not having to go into Durban for bunkers, but when the comparative capital costs were taken into consideration and the availability of bunkers he still felt steam served the company needs best. Always honest in his views, he noted in 1932 that oil and coal price levels in the Depression were such that ANGLO-CANADIAN was more profitable than her steam sisters.

Probably the greatest exponents of the diesel were Scandinavian owners with no home coal supplies and often operating in cross trades far from home. Even these owners with experienced diesel engineers made sure their ships carried an ample supply of spares. It has been said their ships sailed from their home ports with the equivalent of a complete engine welded to the engine room bulkheads as spares.

The Annual General Meetings of the company, usually held late in May, were watched with interest as the chairman, in moving the adoption of the

*ANGLO-AUSTRALIAN (2) arriving Vancouver to load, 10 September 1937. Taken from Prospect Point as she entered the First Narrows, Lions Gate.*
*(Vancouver Maritime Museum Collection)*

report and accounts, would give an address ranging over current shipping and general matters. In the decade following The Great War Sir John Latta expressed his views on taxation, the growing power of unions and in 1925 reviewed Communism. In part he said —

"It is my profound belief that the present so-called capitalistic system, in the heavy national obligations it has to bear, while far too burdensome on the enterprising ambitious man, provides the most practicable conception of what Socialists mistakenly imagine their system would yield to the people, both as regards employment and happiness... The experience of Russia has proved that the moment the line between Capitalism and Socialism is crossed, accumulated wealth disappears like a shadow—its foundation being unimpeachable credit, not gold. Thus, Socialism may be compared to a trader without capital..."

*ANGLO-AFRICAN (2) in Sydney Harbour, February 1939. (I.J. Farquhar Collection)*

At the end of the decade Sir Philip Haldin of Court Line stated that all efficient tonnage was employed, but not earning adequate returns. Haldin considered lack of cohesion and inane competition between owners to be the fault. Shortage of cargo on liner trades did little to help tramp rates: in Australia during 1928/1929 one liner seeking to take parcels of bulk cargo to fill empty space precipitated a fall of 7s 6d, another later caused a fall of 5s 0d. The glut of ships was partly due to the building of ships backed by Trade Facility Act guarantees, but mainly because owners anticipated an upturn of trade and placed orders in anticipation. This optimism was based on long experience of shipping trends, but this time it failed to be realised.

With the new ships entering service the older units were placed on the disposal market. First to go, for £11,500, was ANGLO-SAXON in 1926 to become the Italian HUMANITAS. As such she lasted until broken up in 1930. On 12 March 1930 she lost her rudder off Vigo, on passage from Almeria for Rotterdam. This may have resulted from damage sustained on 1 February when she grounded across the channel arriving at West Hartlepool in ballast

ANGLO-SAXON (2) in the Tyne                    (World Ship Photo Library)

from Dunkirk. From Hartlepool she called at Oran and Savona before sailing from Almeria on 8 March. Assistance from other ships, and Vigo tugs, was declined in preference to waiting for the arrival of SAN GIUSEPPE, a member of the same fleet. The tugs SEAMAN and IRISHMAN were then engaged to tow her to Rotterdam where, after arriving on 8 April, she discharged and went to the breakers to whom she had been sold for £6,550 whilst still under tow, Frank Rijsdijk's Industrieele Ondernemingen N.V., Hendrik-Ido-Ambacht. The state of the freight market and the onset of the Depression negated any idea of repairing a ship nearly thirty years old. January 1927 saw ANGLO-MEXICAN become the Italian RESPICE PATRIAM and later MONREALE until broken up in 1932. She realised £28,000 whilst ANGLO-EGYPTIAN went for £41,500 in December when she became the Finnish OLOVSBORG. Seized when Brazil declared war in 1942 and renamed LESTELOIDE she became a Brazilian Navy training ship in 1948 and went to breakers in Rio de Janeiro during 1953.

The Wall Street collapse on "Black Tuesday", 29 October 1929, heralded the Great Depression, and the bottom fell out of the mediocre freight market. The conservative management by Sir John Latta now paid dividends, or rather ensured the continued payment of dividends to shareholders. Many companies were unable to do so, but Nitrate Producers' never passed a set of accounts without a cheque to investors. With these conditions prevailing the company were fortunate to realise £40,000 in 1930 when ANGLO-CHILEAN, now rather too large for company requirements, was sold to the Houston Line. Renamed HERACLIDES she became the London owned HERMES in 1939 only to be seized by Vichy authorities at Algiers in June 1941. Renamed ST FRANCOIS she then became the Italian ALCAMO the following year and, as such, lasted until 25 February 1943. An Italian convoy of two merchant ships and three escorting destroyers had been sighted south of Marettimo Island and was attacked by Wellingtons and Beauforts from Malta. On the night of 24-25 February 1943 a 39 Squadron Beaufort captained by Pilot Officer J.N. Cartwright attacked and damaged ALCAMO with a torpedo, a few hours later Flying Officer S.R. Muller-Rowland, also with a 39 Squadron Beaufort, completed the destruction of ALCAMO with a second torpedo.

*ANGLO-PERUVIAN (2) at Adelaide*                    *(I.J. Farquhar Collection)*

*ANGLO-PERUVIAN (2) discharging Canadian timber at Noumea, July 1938.                 (D. R. Hudson)*

*Firemen and trimmers, ANGLO-PERUVIAN (2). (D. R. Hudson)*

*The boat deck of ANGLO-PERUVIAN (2). (D.R. Hudson)*

*Crossing the line, ANGLO-PERUVIAN (2) July 1938. Neptune comes on board and uses the temporary swimming pool built into the deck cargo for the ceremony.        (D.R. Hudson)*

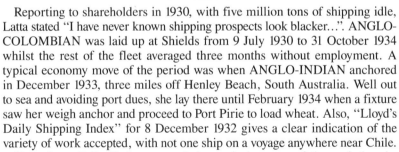

Reporting to shareholders in 1930, with five million tons of shipping idle, Latta stated "I have never known shipping prospects look blacker...". ANGLO-COLOMBIAN was laid up at Shields from 9 July 1930 to 31 October 1934 whilst the rest of the fleet averaged three months without employment. A typical economy move of the period was when ANGLO-INDIAN anchored in December 1933, three miles off Henley Beach, South Australia. Well out to sea and avoiding port dues, she lay there until February 1934 when a fixture saw her weigh anchor and proceed to Port Pirie to load wheat. Also, "Lloyd's Daily Shipping Index" for 8 December 1932 gives a clear indication of the variety of work accepted, with not one ship on a voyage anywhere near Chile.

Years later, D.R. Hudson recorded a typical voyage of the period as he completed his sea time to sit for his second mate's ticket in 1938. Signing on at South Shields, ANGLO-PERUVIAN sailed on 30 April 1938 in ballast bound for British Columbia, where she was to load timber at ports such as Port Alberni, Crofton, New Westminster, Victoria and Port Gamble for Noumea and Melbourne. Clearing British Columbia on 25 June 1938 she was at Noumea between 21 and 23 July and Melbourne from 2 to 18 August. Completing discharge at Melbourne she bunkered at Newcastle, NSW, before

**Position Report—8 December 1932**

ANGLO-AFRICAN—arrived Galveston 6 December from the Tyne.
ANGLO-AUSTRALIAN—sailed Oran 8 November for Melbourne, passed Cape of Good
    Hope 29 November.
ANGLO-CANADIAN—sailed Seletar 5 December for Sydney.
ANGLO-COLOMBIAN—arrived Tyne 9 July 1930, laid up.
ANGLO-INDIAN—sailed Cardiff 15 November and Falmouth 17 November for Table
    Bay and Sydney, passed Dakar 25 November.
ANGLO-PERUVIAN—sailed Sydney 29 November for Shanghai.
ANGLO-SAXON—sailed Tyne 23 November for Geelong, passed Las Palmas 30
    November.

proceeding to the Philippines to collect a cargo of copra at ports ranging from Zamboanga to Iloilo. The copra was destined for San Francisco, California (22 to 28 October), after which the ship moved north to load scrap at Portland, Oregon (30 October), and logs at Seattle between 12 and 15 November. So far the weather had been kind, but this was to change when she sailed from Seattle for Japan, and faced winter gales of hurricane force. The deck cargo was lost overboard and damage sustained by the ship. The worst of the damage was a fracture of the main deck at the after end of No 3 hatch which caused concern to all on board as the loss of ANGLO-AUSTRALIAN was fresh in mind. All the Yokohama cargo had been lost, so the balance was discharged at Osaka between 27 and 31 December, before repairing at Kobe. Repairs completed, in January 1939 a cargo of soya beans for Hamburg was loaded at Rashin, Korea. Sailing from Rashin on 18 January 1939 a passage of 65 days, transiting the Suez Canal on 13 March and bunkering at Sabang and Algiers, saw her arrival at Hamburg reported on 3 April 1939. Twelve days later ANGLO-PERUVIAN sailed in ballast for the Tyne, arriving on 18 April where Hudson took his discharge nearly a year after signing on.

Latta was outspoken against subsidies, both foreign and British. He deprecated the building of tonnage with Trade Facility Act guarantees in the 1920s even though he had made use of them himself, and when the British Shipping (Assistance) Act, 1935—better known as the "Scrap and Build" scheme—was introduced in 1935 he termed it visionless and interference. He later wrote, in June 1939 —

> "I have studied shipping in 25 overseas countries, have had a very wide practical experience of both shipbuilding and shipowning and have reached the conclusion that we suffer as much from incompetence in the management of our ships as we do from foreign subsidised competition... Our chief tramp opponents have been the Greeks yet they have neither subsidies nor Government assistance of any kind."

Having cash reserves when "Scrap and Build" came into effect, consideration was being given to placing orders, but implementation was deferred in light of the government intervention. "Fairplay" latter expressed the opinion that this deferment was a mistake as shipbuilding prices tended to rise in the years that followed. Latta preferred co-operation between owners, on the lines of the tanker agreement known as the Schierwater Plan, financed by owners, and not subsidy. In addition to financing new tonnage the scheme also involved payments to tramp owners of a subsidy for three years if the

ANGLO-INDIAN (2) on trials.                    (World Ship Photo Library)

Tramp freight index fell below a predetermined level. The Nitrate Producers'
Steamship Company therefore received £19,933 in respect of 1935 and £20,679
for 1936. No payments were made for 1937 as the tramp index rose above
the trigger point.

The fleet was reduced by the sale of ANGLO-COLOMBIAN in 1936, and
ANGLO-INDIAN the following year. Only twelve years old, ANGLO-
INDIAN passed to Turnbull, Scott and Company for £50,000 and became
their BAXTERGATE. As such she towed the steamer STANHILL, which had
lost its propeller, some 800 miles into Colombo, and attracted much attention
by towing the casualty into harbour without the aid of tugs. In 1941 she was
one of nine ships at Takoradi which were ordered to sail independently for
Freetown, and was the only one to arrive as all the others were sunk. Passing
through various hands and given the names ARTYGIA, DOMINA and LILY
MICHALOS she was one of the last survivors of the fleet when she went
to Hong Kong breakers in 1959.

The following year saw the entry into service of a new ANGLO-INDIAN.
Launched on 18 November 1937 she was built to Isherwood's new
"Arcform"—Short Brothers also built ARCWEAR, the first ship to this design,
in 1934—as well as the older longitudinal system and was the first "Arcform"
ship to be fitted with the latest North Eastern Marine "Reheater" triple
expansion machinery. The greatest source of thermal inefficiency in
reciprocating machinery was caused by condensation of steam. This had been
partially overcome by superheating, keeping the steam dry for much longer.
North Eastern Marine inserted a heat exchanger (the "Reheater") between
the high and intermediate pressure cylinders. Steam from the boiler entered
the exchanger at 750°F and left to enter the high pressure cylinder at 600°F.
Leaving the high pressure cylinder steam passed through the other side of
the exchanger and had its temperature raised by 140-200°F before proceeding
through the other two cylinders to the condenser. This simple layout gave a
further 10% economy over superheating. Becoming Reardon Smith's
TACOMA CITY after the final fleet sale she then carried the names
INCHCASTLE and LUCKY before Taiwanese shipbreakers claimed her in
1969.

In 1924 Sir John Latta's only son, Cecil Latta, joined the office after completing his education at Oxford University. Elected a member of the Baltic Exchange in 1927 he became a director of the companies and, during 1931, visited Canada and made a trip through the Panama Canal on one of the fleet. A progressive young man, he frequently made use of the aeroplane as a mode of travel. Sadly, whilst in Paris, he died of heart failure on 26 December 1937.

The other tragedy of the period was the loss of ANGLO-AUSTRALIAN which sailed from Cardiff in ballast bound for British Columbia on 8 March 1938 under the command of Captain Parslow, who had been on the bridge with his father during the attack by U39 on ANGLO-CALIFORNIAN in 1915. Promoted to command of ANGLO-COLOMBIAN in 1924 he took ANGLO-AUSTRALIAN twelve years later. The last news from ANGLO-AUSTRALIAN was a wireless message on 14 March when passing Fayal stating "All Well". Posted missing at Lloyd's on 11 May it was assumed she foundered north west of Fayal. The general conclusion of the subsequent Court of Inquiry was that she broke in two during heavy weather as did the Greek MOUNT KYLLENE in the same area on 9 April. It is known she suffered from structural weakness and the shelter deck was prone to develop cracks which were regularly welded. This rather reminds us of the more recent loss of DERBYSHIRE and shows the change in attitudes that have taken place. In 1938 the owners were held blameless, would they have been so today? As a postscript a decade later, in January 1948, the Liberty ship SAMKEY, managed by the New Zealand Shipping Company for the Ministry of Transport, went missing in the same area.

Captain Frederick Parslow, DSC.

ANGLO-CANADIAN (2) at Lyttelton.
(I.J. Farquhar collection)

# WORLD WAR II                                    *9*

War clouds again loomed on the horizon. By early 1939 all British ships had received Envelope Z addressed to "The Master", and inscribed "Not to be opened until instructed by wireless message". Chamberlain had bought breathing time at Munich, knowing war was inevitable and that the country was in no way ready. The needs of industry as the rearmament programme got under way provided cargo for British shipping. On breaking the imposing Admiralty seal on Sunday morning, 3 September, masters found the brief contents confirmed instructions given on the Defence Course many had attended, gave a new secret call sign for the ship, forbade wireless transmission except in emergency and ordered the avoidance of frequented shipping routes.

In September 1939 Nitrate Producers' went to war for a second time, with a fleet of five ships, half the number of 1914. Sadly VJ Day in 1945 failed to see the attractive markings of the fleet resumed as two years previously the houseflag and burgee had been bundled into the flag locker for the last time. On 3 September 1939 only one of the fleet was in European waters, ANGLO-AFRICAN arriving at Liverpool the following day from Australia. ANGLO-SAXON was in port at Cape Town, arriving on 2 September and sailing on the 5th, on passage from Fremantle for Avonmouth. The other three were all in the Pacific. ANGLO-PERUVIAN had sailed from Port Kembla on 23 August for Konan (North Korea) where she arrived on 14 October—3 September found her two-thirds of the way to Makatea where she reported on 8 September. ANGLO-CANADIAN was homeward bound, sailing from Vancouver on 24 August. The outbreak of war found her well on the way to the Panama Canal through which she transited to arrive at Panama on 10 September. After calling at Kingston, Jamaica, she arrived at Liverpool on 12 October. ANGLO-INDIAN had also been on the North Pacific coast, sailing on 13 August from Portland, Oregon, for Australia. Calling at Honolulu on 23 August, it was 13 September before she was reported arriving at Melbourne. Continuing westward via Cape Town she reached the Tyne on Christmas Eve.

Learning from the lessons of 1914-1918 Government policy was to take all ships on charter and retain their owners as managers. Rates would be set to ensure reasonable returns and avoid exorbitant profits which would then be clawed back by excess profits taxes. The Anglo fleet were all taken over, as follows:

ANGLO-AFRICAN    28. 7.1940 to  2. 3.1946
ANGLO-CANADIAN 19. 4.1940 to 25. 6.1942**
ANGLO-INDIAN     8. 1.1940 to  2. 5.1946
ANGLO-PERUVIAN 16. 6.1940 to 23. 2.1941**
ANGLO-SAXON     28. 3.1940 to  2.11.1942**
    ** charter ceased as ship lost.

69

**William E. Ellis (1910-1984)**
Photograph taken at Cardiff, November 1939, when 2nd officer of ANGLO-SAXON. His service with Lawther, Latta and Company commenced as apprentice on ANGLO-AUSTRALIAN in 1927 and ended when he signed off ANGLO-SAXON in May 1940.

His brother-in-law was Alun Lewis (1915-1944), who nearly joined him in the Merchant Navy in May 1940. Instead Lewis, a promising soldier-poet and writer of World War II, joined the Royal Engineers and rose to be a Captain in the South Wales Borderers when he died of wounds in the Burma Campaign.

Ellis was later chief officer of FORT ATHABASKA which was at Bari when the harbour was attacked by the Luftwaffe on 2 December 1943. Ashore at a cinema he returned to find his ship sunk and only ten survivors from the crew of 56.

With Allied Forces advancing on Rome, Bari was an important supply port with over 30 ships discharging. The urgent need of supplies was such the harbour lights were on when more than a hundred Ju88 bombers took the defences by surprise. Eighteen ships, including five Liberties, were sunk. Ammunition ships blew up, oil and petrol fires spread through the harbour. One ship that blew up was JOHN HARVEY, whose cargo included 100 tons of mustard gas bombs. Liquid mustard gas spread across the harbour. Over 1,000 died and 800 were admitted to hospital, gas being responsible for many of the casualties.

Although gas was not used in World War II, supplies were kept ready by the Allies in case Axis forces made a gas attack. On two occasions gas was released, at Bari and when EMPIRE SAILOR was sunk by U518 on 21 November 1942. Her cargo included 270 tons of phosgene and mustard gas, some of which was released. Of her crew 22 died, most from gas.

The company suffered heavily at sea, three of the ships being lost to enemy action, as was the managed EMPIRE SUNRISE. The crews of these four ships totalled 188 and of these 69 were lost.

First, and most terrible, was the loss of ANGLO-SAXON, outward bound from Newport with coal for Bahia Blanca. The first command of Philip Flynn, who had been promoted from mate of ANGLO-CANADIAN to take her in August 1937, she had already been brought to the notice of the Committee of Lloyd's and was due to be posted missing, untraced, when, at the end of October 1940, two emaciated figures staggered ashore on the Island of Eleuthera after drifting 2,500 miles in 71 days. That drift started after night had fallen in mid-Atlantic, 800 miles west of the Canaries, when all hell broke loose as a German raider announced her presence with a smothering rain of gunfire followed by a torpedo.

The unwelcome stranger was WIDDER. Built in 1930 as the Hamburg America Line NEUMARK she had been converted into an armed merchant cruiser by Blohm and Voss. Renamed WIDDER, she sailed from Kiel on 5 May 1940 under the command of Korvettenkapitän Hellmuth von Ruckteschell.

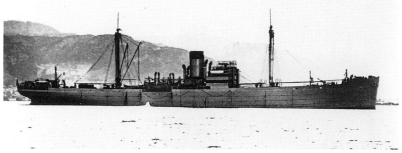

*German auxiliary cruiser HSK3 or WIDDER* (WS Bilddienst)

Seven ships fell victim to her, including the only deep sea sailing ship to be sunk by the World War II German raiders (the Finnish KILLORAN), before ANGLO-SAXON was sighted. Von Ruckteschell had developed his method of attack, aiming to silence the defensive armament of his victims before they could damage WIDDER and to prevent the transmission of any distress signals. Having sighted a target a fast approach in the dark, heavy fire from the raider's six 15cm (5.9 inch) guns, supported by lighter weapons, brought a rapid conclusion to such encounters.

In 26°10′N 34°09′W, at 8pm on 21 August 1940, the first salvo landed on ANGLO-SAXON, four shells on the poop blowing up her ready use ammunition stowed close to her gun. When the radio started sending signals heavy fire swept her decks and a torpedo hastened the end. Dawn found a

*Wilbert Widdicombe and Robert Tapscott sail the jolly boat in Nassau Harbour after their ordeal. The boat is now in the care of Mystic Seaport Museum.*

lifeboat with seven survivors led by the mate, Barry Denny. Three weeks later only two were left, Wilbert Widdicombe (who was at the wheel when the attack started) and Robert Tapscott. On 29 October they landed, gaunt and blackened by the sun, on Eleuthera to be found the following day by a farmer and taken to hospital in Nassau. WIDDER meantime completed her cruise and limped into Brest on 31 October with her turbines in poor shape.

Widdicombe went to sea again and was lost when SIAMESE PRINCE was sunk with all hands by U69 on 17 February 1941. Von Ruckteschell finished the war as German Naval Attache in Tokyo. Returning to Germany he was charged as a war criminal and brought before a military court in May 1947, accused of shelling survivors in lifeboats, including those from ANGLO-SAXON. Found guilty and sentenced to seven years in prison he died there on 24 September 1948. The only raider captain to be accused of war crimes the findings and sentence have led to much discussion, authorities on both sides feeling he should not have been charged. WIDDER also survived the war, lasting until 1955 when wrecked in Maloy Sound as the German FECHENBAUM. Robert Tapscott also survived the war, married in 1949 and died in September 1963, aged 42. He never spoke of his ordeal, his wife and daughter only learning of it shortly before his death.

The next loss was ANGLO-PERUVIAN, with a coal cargo loaded on the Tyne and bound for Boston. Commanded by Captain Cyril Quick, she joined convoy OB288 sailing from Loch Ewe on 21 February 1941. The following day a FW200 Condor from I/KG40 sighted the ships steaming westward. Ten German and Italian submarines were deployed against the convoy, the first sinkings taking place late on 23 February. Amongst these was ANGLO-PERUVIAN hit in the engine room at 9pm by two torpedoes, credited to U95 and Kapitänleutnant Gerd Schreiber. On 24 February the convoy scattered but sinkings continued until ten ships of 52,875 tons had been dispatched. Twenty nine of the crew were lost with ANGLO-PERUVIAN, seventeen survivors being picked up by HARBERTON and landed at Halifax on 4 March. Amongst those lost was Captain Quick. ANGLO-PERUVIAN was to be his first and only command, taken over on 2 January 1941 weeks before he died with her, although he had served on board as second and first mate since 1933.

Two additions were made to the fleet. The Danish motorship ASTORIA was briefly listed in one issue of Lloyd's Confidential Index as being managed for the Ministry of Shipping. I have been unable to confirm this from any other source, so have my reservations whether she was actually taken under management. But in 1941 the EMPIRE SUNRISE, newly completed by Thompson's Sunderland yard for the Ministry of War Transport was taken over and operated under Ministry instructions. When the Tonnage Replacement Scheme was introduced, under which owners were allocated Government owned tonnage to manage and then purchase after the war to replace war losses, she was allocated to Cairns, Noble and Company Ltd, Newcastle, for their Cairn Line of Steamships Ltd, but before she could be transferred by Lawther, Latta and Company, she was lost. Only eighteen months old, heavily laden with 10,000 tons of steel and timber loaded at Three Rivers, she joined convoy SC107 after leaving Sydney, NS, on 28 October 1942. The 42 ship convoy was sighted off Cape Race by U522 and the "Veilchen" patrol line of U-boats moved to intercept. A running contest between attackers and escorts commenced, the first loss being EMPIRE SUNRISE damaged by U402 (Korvettenkapitän Freiherr Siegfried von Forstner) on 2 November, shortly after midnight. Hit forward she kept going for two hours before stopping, being abandoned half an hour later at 2.35am. When last seen, well down by the head and with the main deck awash, it was considered she could be saved, but when a tug arrived from St John's, Newfoundland, only wreckage was sighted. She had been given the coup de grâce by U84 (Kapitänleutnant Horst Uphoff). All the crew, 47 men plus 4 gunners, were saved. The attack on the convoy continued until 6 November with the loss of 15 ships of 82,817 tons.

The Nitrate Boats were also involved in the Far East war with Japan. Japanese Imperial expansion policy logically, with the United States replacing Russia as their main rival, led to the attack on Pearl Harbor (7 December 1941), followed by Japanese advances like a tidal wave across South East Asia and the Pacific. One important prize was possession of the oilfields in the Dutch East Indies, the strategic importance of which was apparent to the Japanese Government with no source of supply under their control. But, like a wave, the initial force was soon dissipated although it took nearly four years to achieve Allied victory. As Vice-Admiral Nagumo attacked Pearl Harbor other forces followed up with invasions of the Philippines and Malaysia. Outnumbered, the Allied forces fell back.

Off Singapore ANGLO-CANADIAN was attacked with bombs and torpedoes by Japanese aircraft. Early in the action a bomb hit the storeroom aft containing the magazine, which was soon ablaze. Chief Officer Beavis and Carpenter Bergstrom led fire fighting efforts and the removal of ammunition whilst above them gun crews remained in action. The following

day when berthed at Singapore an unexploded bomb was discovered in the debris. Captain Williams, with the help of Beavis and Bergstrom, carried it ashore to waste ground where it later exploded. The three received the OBE, MBE and BEM respectively, also Lloyd's War Medals. The BEM also went to Greasers Dunn and Hayes and the DSM to Gunlayer Watson and Corporal Charlton.

The last member of the fleet, ANGLO-INDIAN, was also damaged by bombing at Singapore, on

*Lloyd's War Medal for Bravery at Sea.*

2 February 1942, when one life was lost. Her experiences were later recorded by Arthur McArdle, a Mess Room Steward and Seaman Gunner. He had gone to sea in 1937, aged 15, on ships running the Spanish Civil War blockade, and already knew what it was to be bombed.

McArdle joined ANGLO-INDIAN, commanded by Captain Day, at Blyth, ready to sail on 13 March 1941 with coal for Montevideo. She then loaded grain at Rosario and Buenos Aires and cleared the Plate early in May. Sailing alone she put into St. Vincent, CVI, on 24 May, along with other ships, due to enemy submarine activity and the hunt for the BISMARCK (HMS HOOD had been sunk on 24 May). It was to be 14 June before the assembled ships sailed at night to join a homeward convoy. ANGLO-INDIAN completed the passage at London where she arrived on 10 July. McArdle's second voyage took general cargo and aircraft to Montreal, returning to Manchester with timber.

On 29 September 1941 ANGLO-INDIAN was taken OHMS, loading at Birkenhead a mixed cargo of army supplies, Quads and 25 pounder field guns, Bren gun carriers, motor cycles, ammunition and bombs for the Far East, plus two locomotives for the Indian State Railway. Three Royal Artillery sergeants joined to maintain the equipment during the voyage, and of these Sergeant French was killed by a bomb on the quay alongside the ship at Singapore.

ANGLO-INDIAN sailed from the Mersey on 25 October, called at Durban for fuel and then went to Bombay to land the locomotives. At Durban was a convoy with troops for Singapore, the soldiers destined to become prisoners within days of arrival. Leaving Bombay on 16 January 1942, ANGLO-INDIAN passed through the Sunda Straits and joined a convoy from Australia which included GORGON and PHRONTIS, escorted by the cruiser HOBART and destroyers, arriving at Singapore on 1 February.

Japanese attacks had started after passing the Banka Strait, and these continued after berthing with the aid of ratings from the lost PRINCE OF WALES. Despite the presence of a platoon of Ghurkas the dockers did little and after the first day were not seen again. Discharge was carried out by the crew and troops, as equipment was landed it was rushed away straight into action. In the incessant bombing ANGLO-INDIAN was fortunate in not receiving a direct hit, but blast damage from near misses and shrapnel caused much damage and left a large hole in the starboard quarter. At times, during raids, ANGLO-INDIAN lay off the quay, returning to wherever discharge could continue despite the chaos and burning sheds. Finally, at night, she sneaked out on 5 February on one serviceable boiler, reaching Batavia three days later.

Captain Day was asked to tow a submarine or destroyer to safety, but with the damage sustained and a list to port was unable to comply. Sailing from Batavia on 12 February, three days before Singapore fell, what was left of the cargo was discharged at Colombo before ANGLO-INDIAN proceeded to Karachi for repairs. Finally, loading a cargo of hides and bonemeal, she sailed on 18 March via the Cape for Liverpool, arriving on 18 May and coming off OHMS on 3 June. McArdle signed off on 19 May, ending his service with ANGLO-INDIAN.

Singapore fell to the Japanese on 15 February 1942. Two days previous the steamer KUNG WO attempted to escape only to be bombed later in the day some 80 miles out. Amongst her passengers was a young RN lieutenant, Geoffrey Brooke, who later recorded his wartime career in "Attack Starboard". A survivor from the battleship PRINCE OF WALES, sunk with the battle cruiser REPULSE by Japanese aircraft on 10 December 1941, he reached the coast of Sumatra 30 miles away and, with other refugees, travelled up the Indragiri River to cross the island and reach Padang.

Before Japanese forces reached Padang Brooke, along with fifteen other officers, a Chinese and a Malay, put to sea on 8 March 1942 on board the 45ft prauw SEDERHANA DJOHANIS in an endeavour to reach India. Five weeks later they met ANGLO-CANADIAN and caught up with events.

Having engulfed Malaya and Indonesia the Japanese tidal wave swept on into the Indian Ocean and Bay of Bengal, with submarines ranging to the coast of Africa. Warned by intelligence, shipping was ordered out of ports from Calcutta to Colombo. Those unable to get clear of the area were to pay a heavy price as late in March Nagumo led his Pearl Harbor fleet towards Ceylon and the remaining British fleet. At the same time Vice-Admiral Ozawa led another force deep into the Bay of Bengal to destroy shipping and provide

*ANGLO-CANADIAN (2) seen from SENDERHANA DJOHANIS off Ceylon.*

*(G. Brooke)*

a diversion from the much larger force to the south.

Heavy losses had been sustained by the Allied fleet on 27 February at the Battle of the Java Sea. To these were added the cruisers DORSETSHIRE and CORNWALL, sunk by carrier based aircraft on 5 April, and the carrier HERMES four days later. All along the Indian coast distress calls were being monitored as the cruisers and aircraft of Ozawa's three groups rampaged along the coast. Aircraft from the carrier RYUJO raided Vizagapatnam where they found ANGLO-CANADIAN at anchor. Hit by bombs on 6 April and set on fire she was fortunately not badly damaged.

SEDERHANA DJOHANIS survived a machine gun attack by a Japanese bomber on 28 March, later sighting tankers in the distance which failed to respond to their signals. This was fortunate as they were part of the Japanese supply train and another prauw which was sighted by them had its crew of refugees taken prisoner. Later, on 9 April, the sounds of battle were heard to the north, later found to be HERMES and her attendant destroyer VAMPIRE being attacked and sunk by Japanese aircraft. At last, with the Ceylon coast in sight, a steamer was also sighted to the north.

ANGLO-CANADIAN had sailed from Vizagapatnam on 11 April 1942, bound the United Kingdom. Steaming through the wreckage of HERMES and VAMPIRE she sighted SEDERHANA DJOHANIS on 14 April, took off the crew and landed them at Bombay. She had only a few months to survive. After Bombay (arrived 19 April and sailed 25 April), she was reported at Mombasa (5 to 7 May), Dar-es-Salaam (8 to 22 May), Table Bay (1 to 3 June) and was off Ascension Island on 12 June. Leaving Ascension on the next leg of her passage, for Baltimore in ballast, ANGLO-CANADIAN was sighted by Korvettenkapitän Wilfried Reichmann (U153) in 25°12'N 55°31'W. Hit by a torpedo, she sank with the loss of the wireless operator; the rest of the crew, 49 men, reached Anguilla in two lifeboats. Having been taken OHMS at Liverpool in November 1941 she had been continually employed in the Middle East, visiting ports from Cape Town to Haifa, Bombay and Singapore before proceeding south round the Cape of Good Hope to the unscheduled meeting with U153.

Fortunately for the Allies the Japanese sortie into the Bay of Bengal and Indian Ocean proved to be the high-water mark of the tidal wave. Within a

month of ANGLO-CANADIAN picking up the refugees the Battle of the Coral Sea started Japanese reverses. Losses sustained by the Imperial Japanese Navy there and at the crucial Battle of Midway in June 1942 saw most of the ships, aircraft and crews who had attacked Pearl Harbor and forayed into theIndian Ocean destroyed. The slow push back had started, culminating in the signing of the surrender in Tokyo Bay in August 1945.

*Greaser Charles Williams, ANGLO-SAXON August 1940, lost with the ship.* *(Mrs. O. Dunn)*

In the London office Sir John Latta had no successor with the death of his son on Boxing Day 1937. This was followed by news from Belfast of the death of Robert Lawther on 22 March 1941, aged 75. The Nitrate Producers' Steamship Company was to become a company founded, built up and terminated by one man, John Latta.

With heavy loss of life and only two ships left, with both his son and partner dead, Sir John Latta looked at the future and saw nothing. Sadly he came to the conclusion it was time to shut the office so on 27 November 1942 the decision was made to wind up the company and sell the ships. The circular to shareholders from the directors explained they had been influenced in this decision by "... the conditions now prevailing ..." and —

"... the fact that your chairman, Sir John Latta, Bart, who has controlled the management of the business and through whose personal influence such exceptionally satisfactory results have been achieved, is advancing in years and that there is a lack of a successor quite able to take his place when he relinquishes his activities."

A buyer was found in Sir William Reardon Smith and Sons Ltd, Cardiff, who paid £125,000 for ANGLO-AFRICAN and £164,000 for ANGLO-INDIAN early in 1943. ANGLO-INDIAN was later employed as a storeship serving the British sector in the Normandy landings, arriving off the beaches in convoy ETM18 on 27 June 1943. Under wartime regulations it was not permissible to rename ships so they retained their original names until 1948 when they became NEW WESTMINSTER CITY and TACOMA CITY respectively. The subsequent career of ANGLO-INDIAN has been mentioned,

*LUCKY, ex ANGLO-INDIAN (2), discharging bagged cement at Da Nang, July 1969,*
*(W.A. Schell)*

*LORD CODRINGTON, ex ANGLO-AFRICAN (2).* *(World Ship Photo Library)*

the last ship of the fleet to survive. ANGLO-AFRICAN later carried the names LORD CODRINGTON, TOZAI MARU No 7 and RISSHUN MARU No 3 before being broken up in Japan in 1965.

A brief examination of the last balance sheet, for April 1942, shows clearly the healthy state of the business. The ships had been depreciated and stood at only £45,507, compared with the £289,000 received on their sale, with £478,788 in investments and £463,000 on deposit with the bank. Compensation of £75,000 was paid to Lawther, Latta and Company Ltd for loss of management, £30,000 to the staff and £20,000 to the directors for loss of office. Shareholders were told to anticipate receiving £28 immediately for each £5 share, with a further £7 to follow when realisation of assets was completed. Twice in the history of the enterprise a return of this size had been paid to investors. It is unlikely a third such payment would have been possible had the company continued trading after World War II. Although British tramp shipping enjoyed an Indian summer aided by the Korean War and closure of the Suez Canal in 1956, the changing international political scene, the breakup of the Empire, decline in the coal industry (replaced by oil) and introduction of specialist tonnage such as the bulk carrier, flags of convenience and third world crewing would have led to the demise of the company by the middle of the 1970s. By that time some of the smaller companies had been able to withdraw from shipping with their finances intact, but others collapsed with heavy losses.

Sir John Latta enjoyed only a brief retirement, although he was happy to witness the return of peace in 1945. Having worked until he was 75 he survived to the age of 79, dying on 6 December 1946. His partner, Sir Andrew Latta, KBE, survived his brother, dying at his Edinburgh home on 10 August 1953.

In Belfast the Lawther name survived. Following the death of Stanley Lawther in 1929 the post of Group Managing Director fell to the lot of Robert Lawther's son-in-law, Flight Lieutenant Llewellyn R. Briggs who had married Mary Lawther in 1923. The Irish Sea activities were amalgamated during 1929

## Simplified Balance Sheet, 30 April 1942

| | | |
|---|---:|---:|
| To Issued Capital— | | |
| Ordinary shares of £5 each | | £156,300 |
| ,, Capital reserve account | | 446,333 |
| ,, Insurance Fund | | 14,827 |
| ,, Special emergency and taxation reserve account, including capital profit on realised assets | | 276,920 |
| ,, Uncompleted voyages — receipts in excess of disbursements | | 26,870 |
| ,, Sundry creditors | | 31,219 |
| ,, Profit and loss account | | 49,647 |
| | | £1,002,116 |
| By Original cost of vessels | £350,164 | |
| Less depreciation | 304,656 | |
| | | £45,508 |
| ,, Investments at cost | | 478,788 |
| ,, Unexpired insurances | | 6,356 |
| ,, Sundry debtors | | 5,704 |
| ,, Cash at bankers | | 465,760 |
| | | £1,002,116 |

John Latta,  
Thos. S. Short, } Directors  
Wm. V. Smith, Secretary

into a new company, the Belfast, Mersey and Manchester Steamship Company Ltd, which continued to compete with the Belfast Steamship Company until 1944 when an offer from Coast Lines Ltd (already the owners of the Belfast Steamship Company) was accepted and the three companies, S. Lawther and Company Ltd, the Belfast, Mersey and Manchester Steamship Company Ltd and J. and J. Mack, Liverpool, became subsidiaries of the Belfast Steamship Company at a price of £200,000. The services of the two fleets were rationalised but continued to operate independently until the end of 1959 when the Belfast, Mersey and Manchester Steamship Company was merged into the Belfast Steamship Company. As part of the Coast Lines Group they passed to the control of the Peninsular and Oriental Steam Navigation Company in August 1971.

In August 1945, the Briggs family left Belfast and the remaining interests were sold, initially to Maurice May, FCA MP, the Group Company Secretary. The Mersey Coal Company, remembered as a small business conducted with a one horse, two ton van driven by James Officer, passed to another coal merchant, Arthur S. Davidson Ltd, which in due course was itself absorbed by Cawoods Fuels and hence is now part of British Fuels. Lawther and Harvey (they became ''Ltd'' in 1948) continued independent, in 1954 becoming the Northern Ireland agents for the world's first integrated container operation, Anglo-Continental Container Services. Amongst the ships employed in this service was the CLIPPER, built in 1956 and claimed to be the first vessel built for the exclusive carriage of containers. In this role the Lawther name continued the long tradition of competing with the Belfast Steamship Company. In 1966 Lawther and Harvey Ltd followed Anglo-Continental into ownership by the National Freight Company, and after the business merged into Northern Ireland Carriers in

1982 ceased to be an active trading company. Following the 1982 merger the senior staff of Lawther and Harvey Ltd formed a new company, Campbell McCleave and Company Ltd which is today active in the traditional Lawther shipping and transport fields.

Today, memories of the Anglo Line have grown dim, with few who sailed the ships surviving to recall them. In Cumnock a few reminders remain of his role as a benefactor to his home town. In 1925 Latta Crescent was built and during 1930 he established the Rector's Honours Fund and "Dux Medal" at his old school, Cumnock Academy. Other gifts included wayside seats in 1925 and funds for the Order of the Eastern Star (the ladies' section of the Masonic order) to arrange annual outings for old people. With the passage of time and inflation the sum available for these outings dwindled in real terms until, in 1984, court permission was obtained to realise and expend the capital investment on the charitable works of the Order.

*ANGLO-AUSTRALIAN (2)*                     *(World Ship Photo Library)*

# FLEET LIST
# &
# APPENDIX

## Notes on Fleet List

The period in fleet service is indicated after the name. Details then include official number, gross, net and deadweight tonnages, registered dimensions (length, beam and depth) and type of construction (all ships were built of steel). Tonnages are when joining the fleet and could vary considerably with little change to the vessel (viz: ANGLO-CHILEAN 9097 to 7137gt). Deadweight would change if load line regulations were amended, whether shelter deck vessels were open or closed, and also varied according to season and area of the world, and can be quoted with or without allowance for fuel and stores. Dimensions are in feet and tenths, followed by overall length (loa) if known. Two depths are given for spar deck steamers, to main deck and, the larger figure, spar deck. For shelter deck vessels the depth is to main deck, add approximately 8ft for depth to shelter deck. The type of machinery (T = triple expansion, Q = quadruple expansion) is followed by the number of cylinders, engine builders, cylinder bores and stroke (in Imperial or metric measurements according to which would have been used by the builders), number of boilers and working pressure (pounds per square inch), power (ihp = indicated horse power for reciprocating engines, bhp = brake horse power for internal combustion) and speed. Power and speed will vary with quality of bunkers, loading of ship, the extent to which the hull is fouled by marine growth and weather. The figures quoted are as declared on the transcript of ownership issued by the Registrar of Ships. The dates laid down, launched and completed are as noted in the records of Short Brothers. Changes of ownership under the British flag are as recorded by the Registrar, foreign ownership as recorded in Lloyd's Confidential Index. Details of final end are from the records of Lloyd's Register of Shipping and Lloyd's of London.

# Nitrate Producers' Steamship Company Ltd

## 1. COLONEL J. T. NORTH (1895-1897)
ON: 104860. 2835gt 1793nt 4200dwt. 302.1 x 44.8 x 16.4/23.3ft. Spar deck.
T.3-cyl. engine by W. Allan & Co Ltd, Sunderland. Cylinders 23''/38''/62'' x 42'' stroke. 2 boilers, 160lb pressure. 1250ihp. Speed 10 knots.
21.7.1894: laid down. 24.1.1895: launched by Short Bros, Sunderland (Yard No: 239). 4.5.1895: completed for Nitrate Producers' S.S. Co Ltd (Lawther, Latta & Co, managers), London. 1897: sold to G. Racich & Co, Ragusa, Austro-Hungary, renamed ISTOK. 1899: transferred to Navigazione a Vapore Unione (G. Racich, manager), Dubrovnik, Austro-Hungary. 4.8.1914: seized by Russian forces at Taganrog. 24.12.1914: scuttled as a blockship at Zonguldak.

## 2. AVERY HILL (1895-1899)
ON: 105711. 3142gt 2020nt 5130dwt. 351.4 x 42.1 x 17½/25.4ft. Spar deck.
T.3-cyl. engine by G. Clark Ltd, Sunderland. Cylinders 24½''/40''/66'' x 45'' stroke. 2 boilers, 160lb pressure. 1500ihp. Speed 10 knots.
12.1.1895: laid down. 6.6.1895: launched by Short Bros, Sunderland (Yard No: 247). 10.8.1895: completed for Nitrate Producers' S.S. Co Ltd (Lawther, Latta & Co, managers), London. 1899: sold to Dunedin S.S. Co Ltd (Henderson & McIntosh, managers), Leith, renamed DUNEARN. 26.8.1908: capsized and sank off Goto Island while on a voyage from Karatzu for Singapore with a cargo of coal.

## 3. JUANITA NORTH (1896-1906)
ON: 105847. 3503gt 2233nt 5660dwt. 352.0 x 45.0 x 17.2/25.1ft. Spar deck.
T.3-cyl. engine by G. Clark Ltd, Sunderland. Cylinders 24½''/40''/66'' x 45'' stroke. 2 boilers, 180lb pressure. 1500ihp. Speed 10 knots.
21.12.1895: laid down. 13.5.1896: launched by Short Bros, Sunderland (Yard No: 253). 11.7.1896: completed for Nitrate Producers' S.S. Co Ltd (Lawther, Latta & Co, managers), London. 1906: sold to Clapham S.S. Co Ltd (G.E. Macarthy, manager), Newcastle, renamed ELMSGARTH. 1914: transferred to L. Macarthy, Newcastle. 1915: transferred to Garth Shipping Co Ltd (L. Macarthy, manager), Newcastle. 29.9.1917: torpedoed and sunk by U61, 50 miles NW½W of Tory Island while on a voyage from Jamaica and Matanzas for Liverpool with a cargo of sugar.

## 4. GEORGE FLEMING (1897-1911)
ON: 108234. 3448gt 2228nt 5800dwt. 353.0 x 45.0 x 17.2/25.1ft. Spar deck.
T.3-cyl. engine by G. Clark Ltd, Sunderland. Cylinders 24½''/40''/66'' x 45'' stroke. 2 boilers, 180lb pressure. 1500ihp. Speed 10 knots.
26.12.1896: laid down. 14.5.1897: launched by Short Bros, Sunderland (Yard No: 266). 24.7.1897: completed for Nitrate Producers' S.S. Co Ltd (Lawther, Latta & Co, managers), London. 1911: sold to Lloyd del Pacifico S.A. di Nav, Savona, Italy, renamed AFFINITA. 1932: laid up at Genoa, sold and broken up there.

*GEORGE FLEMING*              *(Bibliothek Für Zeitgaschichte, Stuttgart)*

## 5. ANGLO-CHILIAN (1898-1911)
ON: 110004. 3817gt 2442nt 6200dwt. 369.5 x 46.1 x 19.8/27.8ft. Spar deck.
T.3-cyl. engine by G. Clark Ltd, Sunderland. Cylinders 25''/41''/68'' x 48'' stroke. 2 boilers, 180lb pressure. 2000ihp. Speed 10 knots.
30.4.1898: laid down. 3.10.1898: launched by Short Bros, Sunderland (Yard No: 276). 26.11.1898: completed for Nitrate Producers' S.S. Co Ltd (Lawther, Latta & Co, managers), London. 1911: sold to European & Brazilian Shipping Co Ltd (Petersen & Co Ltd, managers), London, renamed RIO IGUASSU. 22.9.1914: captured and sunk by SMS KARLSRUHE in 0°40'S 31°40'W, 155 miles SSW of St Pauls Rock, while on a voyage from the Tyne for Rio de Janeiro with a cargo of coal.

## 6. ANGLO-AUSTRALIAN (1) (1899-1915)
ON: 110121. 4019gt 2581nt 6800dwt. 370.4 x 48.1 x 20.3/28.8ft. Spar deck.
T.3-cyl. engine by G. Clark Ltd, Sunderland. Cylinders 26''/42''/70'' x 48'' stroke. 2 boilers, 180lb pressure. 2000ihp. Speed 12 knots.
1.10.1898: laid down. 28.3.1899: launched by Short Bros, Sunderland (Yard No: 283). 27.5.1899: completed for Nitrate Producers' S.S. Co Ltd (Lawther, Latta & Co, managers), London. 1915: sold to B.J. Sutherland & Co Ltd, Newcastle. 1915: sold to Equinox S.S. Co Ltd (L. Walford (London) Ltd, managers), London, renamed CALONNE. 1919: sold to J.A. Mango, London, renamed BYZANTION (Greek flag). 1921: sold to Steam Nav Co of Samos (D. Inglessi & fils, managers), Samos, Greece, renamed EKATERINA INGLESSI.

83

1926: sold to P.G. Callimanopulos, Piraeus, Greece, renamed EKATERINA C. 28.5.1927: dragged anchors and driven ashore at Kilometre 71, Martin Garcia Channel, River Plate while on a voyage from Piraeus for San Lorenzo in ballast. 1928: arranged total loss. 13.7.1928: refloated, towed to Buenos Aires. 13.3.1929: arrived at Genoa, broken up.

*ANGLO-AFRICAN (1)*

### 7. ANGLO-AFRICAN (1) (1900-1909)

ON: 112770. 4186gt 2693nt 7350dwt. 370.2 x 48.7 x 19.0/28.9ft. Spar deck.
T.3-cyl. engine by G. Clark Ltd, Sunderland. Cylinders 26''/43''/71'' x 51'' stroke. 2 boilers, 180lb pressure. 2250ihp. Speed 11 knots.
25.11.1899: laid down. 24.9.1900: launched by Short Bros, Sunderland (Yard No: 292). 17.11.1900: completed for Nitrate Producers' S.S. Co Ltd (Lawther, Latta & Co, managers), London. 7.1.1909: wrecked 4 miles south of Cape Charles while on a voyage from Tocopilla for Baltimore with a cargo of nitrate.

### 8. ANGLO-CANADIAN (1) (1901-1918)

ON: 114776. 4239gt 2680nt 7000dwt. 380.0 x 50.1 x 19.3/27.9ft. Spar deck.
T.3-cyl. engine by G. Clark Ltd, Sunderland. Cylinders 26½''/44''/73'' x 51'' stroke. 2 boilers, 180lb pressure. 2500ihp. Speed 12 knots.
15.12.1900: laid down. 15.7.1901: launched by Short Bros Ltd, Sunderland (Yard No: 300). 12.10.1901: completed for Nitrate Producers' S.S. Co Ltd (Lawther, Latta & Co, managers), London. 22.1.1918: torpedoed and sunk by KuK U27, 33 miles S½E of Malta while on a voyage from Alexandria for Marseilles with troops.

### 9. ANGLO-PERUVIAN (1) (1905-1906)

ON: 120616. 5494gt 3520nt 9250dwt. 418.2 x 54.4 x 29.3ft. Shelter deck.
Q.4-cyl. engine by Central Marine Engine Works, West Hartlepool. Cylinders 25''/36''/52''/74'' x 54'' stroke. 3 boilers, 216lb pressure. 3000ihp. Speed 11 knots.
2.11.1904: laid down. 3.8.1905: launched by Short Bros Ltd, Sunderland (Yard No: 324). 1.11.1905: completed for Nitrate Producers' S.S. Co Ltd (Lawther, Latta & Co, managers), London. 21.4.1906: struck an iceberg in the North Atlantic while on a voyage from the Tyne for Philadelphia in ballast. 24.4.1906: foundered.

10. **ANGLO-BOLIVIAN**    — see S4

11. **ANGLO-COLOMBIAN (1)**    — see S14

12. **ANGLO-SAXON (1)**    — see S13

13. **SOUTH AMERICA**    — see S3

14. **SOUTH AUSTRALIA**    — see S2

15. **WINKFIELD**    — see S12

*ANGLO-MEXICAN*

### 16. ANGLO-MEXICAN (1908-1927)
ON: 125666. 4796gt 2293nt 8150dwt. 394.0 x 52.4 x 27.9ft. Shelter deck.
Q.4-cyl. engine by North Eastern Marine Engineering Co Ltd, Newcastle.
Cylinders 24"/34"/49"/71" x 48" stroke. 3 boilers, 220lb pressure. 2700ihp.
Speed 11 knots.
19.6.1907: laid down. 7.12.1907: launched by Short Bros Ltd, Sunderland
(Yard No: 342). 11.3.1908: completed for Nitrate Producers' S.S. Co Ltd
(Lawther, Latta & Co, managers), London. 1927: sold to S.A. di Nav "La
Serenissima", Genoa, Italy, renamed RESPICE PATRIAM. 1929: sold to Nav
Alta Italia S.A., Genoa, Italy, renamed MONREALE. 13.2.1932: arrived at
Savona for breaking up.

### 17. ANGLO-PATAGONIAN (1910-1917)
ON: 129120. 5017gt 3104nt 8650dwt. 403.0 x 52.4 x 26.9ft. Shelter deck.
Q.4-cyl. engine by North Eastern Marine Engineering Co Ltd, Newcastle.
Cylinders 24"/34½"/49"/71" x 48" stroke. 3 boilers, 220lb pressure.
2500ihp. Speed 10¾knots.
1.12.1909: laid down. 26.5.1910: launched by Short Bros Ltd, Sunderland (Yard
No: 363). 17.8.1910: completed for Nitrate Producers' S.S. Co Ltd (Lawther,
Latta & Co, managers), London. 10.7.1917: torpedoed and sunk by UC72,
20 miles WSW of Les Sables d'Olonne while on a voyage from New York
for Bordeaux with general cargo and horses.

ANGLO-PATAGONIAN

ANGLO-CALIFORNIAN                              (World Ship Photo Library)

**18.   ANGLO-CALIFORNIAN   (1912-1915)**
ON: 132711. 7333gt 4618nt 10500dwt. 425.0 x 56.3 x 36.3ft. Shelter deck.
Q.4-cyl. engine by North Eastern Marine Engineering Co Ltd, Newcastle.
Cylinders $25\frac{1}{2}''/36\frac{1}{2}''/52\frac{1}{2}''/76''$ x 54'' stroke. 3 boilers, 220lb pressure.
3400ihp. Speed 12 knots.
24.5.1911: laid down. 21.2.1912: launched by Short Bros Ltd, Sunderland (Yard
No: 372). 22.5.1912: completed for Nitrate Producers' S.S. Co Ltd (Lawther,
Latta & Co, managers), London. 1915: sold to Cunard S.S. Co Ltd, Liverpool,
renamed VANDALIA. 9.6.1918: torpedoed and sunk by U96 in 51°44'N
06°10'W while on a voyage from Liverpool for Montreal in ballast.

**19.   ANGLO-EGYPTIAN   (1912-1927)**
ON: 135166. 7379gt 4640nt 11350dwt. 425.0 x 56.3 x 36.3ft. Shelter deck.
Q.4-cyl. engine by North Eastern Marine Engineering Co Ltd, Newcastle.
Cylinders $25\frac{1}{2}''/36\frac{1}{2}''/52\frac{1}{2}''/76''$ x 54'' stroke. 3 boilers, 220lb pressure.
3400ihp. Speed 12 knots.
21.2.1912: laid down. 25.9.1912: launched by Short Bros Ltd, Sunderland (Yard
No: 376). 16.12.1912: completed for Nitrate Producers' S.S. Co Ltd (Lawther,

86

Latta & Co, managers), London. 1927: sold to J.A. Zachariassen & Co (A.G. Zachariassen, manager), Djursholm (Nystad), Finland, renamed OLOVSBORG. 1941: seized by the Brazilian Government. 1942 sold to Lloyd Brasileiro, Rio de Janeiro, renamed LESTELOIDE. 1948: to Brazilian Navy, training ship 91N. 1953: broken up at Rio de Janeiro by Irmaos Almeida.

*A weather-worn ANGLO-EGYPTIAN.* *(World Ship Photo Library)*

### 20. ANGLO-BRAZILIAN (1913-1915)
ON: 135294. 7486gt 4668nt 10500dwt. 425.5 x 56.3 x 28.2ft. Shelter deck.
Q.4-cyl. engine by North Eastern Marine Engineering Co Ltd, Newcastle. Cylinders $25\frac{1}{2}''/36\frac{1}{2}''/52\frac{1}{2}''/76''$ x 54'' stroke. 3 boilers, 220lb pressure. 3400ihp. Speed 12 knots.
28.1.1913: laid down. 2.10.1913: launched by Short Bros Ltd, Sunderland (Yard No: 381). 13.12.1913: completed for Nitrate Producers' S.S. Co Ltd (Lawther,

*ANGLO-BRAZILIAN.* *(I.J. Farquhar Collection)*

Latta & Co, managers), London. 1915: sold to Union-Castle Mail S.S. Co Ltd, London, renamed CHEPSTOW CASTLE. 7.4.1932: dragged anchors while laid up at Rothesay Bay, ashore at Toward Point. Sold and 10.5.1932: arrived at Port Glasgow for breaking up by Smith & Houston Ltd.

*ANGLO-CHILEAN.*                                        *(A. Greenway Collection)*

## 21.  ANGLO-CHILEAN  (1916-1930)
ON: 139163. 9097gt 5799nt 13050dwt. 470.5 x 58.3 x 27.8ft. Shelter deck. Q.4-cyl. engine by G. Clark Ltd, Sunderland. Cylinders 26''/36½''/53''/76'' x 54'' stroke. 3 boilers, 220lb pressure. 3000ihp. Speed 11 knots.
8.12.1914: laid down. 2.5.1916: launched by Short Bros Ltd, Sunderland (Yard No: 390). 30.11.1916: completed for Nitrate Producers' S.S. Co Ltd (Lawther, Latta & Co, managers), London. 1930: sold to British & South American S.N. Co Ltd (Houston Line (London) Ltd, managers), London, renamed HERACLIDES. 1939: sold to Hermes S.S. Co Ltd, London, renamed HERMES. 25.6.1940: seized at Algiers by Vichy Authorities, renamed ST FRANCOIS. 9.12.1942: seized by German forces at Marseilles, transferred to Italy (S.A. di Nav Adriatica, Venice, managers), renamed ALCAMO. 25.2.1943: torpedoed and sunk by Beauforts of 39 Squadron, R.A.F., 73 miles north of Trapani while on a voyage from Bizerta for Naples.

*ANGLO-COLOMBIAN (2) at Adelaide*                      *(I.J. Farquhar Collection)*

## 22. ANGLO-COLOMBIAN (2) (1921-1936)
ON: 143091. 8407gt 5333nt 12175dwt. 479.0 x 62.2 x 33.0ft. Two deck.
Q.4-cyl. engine by builders. Cylinders 720/1030/1480/2170mm x 1400mm
stroke. 4 boilers, 213lb pressure. 3750ihp. Speed 11 knots.
29.5.1915: launched by A.G. Weser, Bremen (Yard No: 207). 10.1915:
completed as SCHWARZENFELS for D.D.G. Hansa, Bremen, Germany.
29.3.1919: arrived U.K. port, surrendered to Allied Shipping Commission and
allocated to Britain, The Shipping Controller (Macvicar, Marshall & Co Ltd,
Liverpool, managers). 1921: purchased by Nitrate Producers' S.S. Co Ltd
(Lawther, Latta & Co Ltd, managers), London, renamed ANGLO-COLOMBIAN.
1936: sold to Atlas Reederei A.G. (Schulte & Bruns, managers), Emden,
Germany, renamed AFRIKA. 21.12.1936: foundered north of Trondheim while
on a voyage from Narvik for Emden with a cargo of iron ore.

*ANGLO-INDIAN (1)*                                                    *(A. Duncan)*

## 23. ANGLO-INDIAN (1) (1925-1937)
ON: 148665. 5531gt 3400nt 10020dwt. 426.0 x 59.5 x 26.0ft. (439.6ft
loa). Shelter deck. Monitor hull.
Q.4-cyl. engine by North Eastern Marine Engineering Co Ltd, Newcastle.
Cylinders $23\frac{1}{2}''/32\frac{1}{2}''/47''/68''$ x 48'' stroke. 3 boilers, 220lb pressure.
2100ihp. Speed $10\frac{1}{2}$ knots.
10.2.1925: laid down. 7.7.1925: launched by Short Bros Ltd, Sunderland (Yard
No: 421). 1.9.1925: completed for Nitrate Producers' S.S. Co Ltd (Lawther,
Latta & Co, managers), London. 1937: sold to Redgate S.S. Co Ltd (Turnbull,
Scott & Co, managers), London, renamed BAXTERGATE. 1947: sold to
Panamanian Tramp Shipping Co S.A., Panama (Stathatos & Co Ltd, London,
managers), renamed ARTYGIA. 1948: sold to Cia de Nav Cabaco S.A.,
Panama, renamed DOMINA. 1955: sold to Mrs L.C. Michalos, Michalos Bros
& others (Michalinos Maritime & Commercial Co Ltd, managers), Piraeus,
Greece, renamed LILY MICHALOS. 21.8.1959: arrived at Hong Kong for
breaking up by H.K. Chiap Hua Manufactory Co (1947) Ltd.

## 24. ANGLO-PERUVIAN (2) (1926-1941)
ON: 149698. 5457gt 3331nt 10138dwt. 426.0 x 58.0 x 26.1ft. (439.5ft loa).
Shelter deck.
Q.4-cyl. engine by North Eastern Marine Engineering Co Ltd, Newcastle.
Cylinders $23\frac{1}{2}''/32\frac{1}{2}''/47''/68''$ x 48'' stroke. 3 boilers, 220lb pressure.
2100ihp. Speed $10\frac{1}{2}$ knots.
19.1.1926: laid down. 10.6.1926: launched by Short Bros Ltd, Sunderland (Yard
No: 423). 30.7.1926: completed for Nitrate Producers' S.S. Co Ltd (Lawther,
Latta & Co Ltd, managers), London. 23.2.1941: torpedoed and sunk by U95
in 59°30'N 21°00'W while on a voyage from the Tyne for Boston with a
cargo of coal.

ANGLO-PERUVIAN (1).                                    (A. Duncan)

ANGLO-AUSTRALIAN (2) at Adelaide.              (I.J. Farquhar Collection)

## 25.  ANGLO-AUSTRALIAN (2)  (1927-1938)
ON: 149817. 5456gt 3332nt 10138dwt. 426.0 x 58.0 x 26.1ft. Shelter deck.
Q.4-cyl. engine by North Eastern Marine Engineering Co Ltd, Newcastle.
Cylinders 23½''/32½'''/47''/68'' x 48'' stroke. 3 boilers, 220lb pressure.
2100ihp. Speed 10½ knots.
2.2.1926: laid down. 21.3.1927: launched by Short Bros Ltd, Sunderland (Yard
No: 424). 4.5.1927: completed for Nitrate Producers' S.S. Co Ltd (Lawther,
Latta & Co Ltd, managers), London. 8.3.1938: sailed Cardiff for Vancouver
in ballast. 14.3.1938: in wireless communication passing Fayal. 11.5.1938:
posted missing at Lloyd's.

## 26.  ANGLO-CANADIAN (2)  (1928-1942)
ON: 160529. 5268gt 3246nt 9746dwt. 426.0 x 58.0 x 24.7ft. (439.8ft
loa). Shelter deck.
4-cyl. single-acting opposed piston diesel by W. Doxford & Sons Ltd,
Sunderland. Cylinders 560mm x 2160mm stroke. 2400bhp. Speed 10½ knots.
15.11.1927: laid down. 3.5.1928: launched by Short Bros Ltd, Sunderland (Yard
No: 430). 23.7.1928: completed for Nitrate Producers' S.S. Co Ltd (Lawther,
Latta & Co Ltd, managers), London. 25.6.1942: torpedoed and sunk by U153
in 25°12'N 55°31'W while on a voyage from Vizagapatnam for Baltimore,
via Ascension, in ballast.

## 27.  ANGLO-SAXON (2)  (1929-1940)
ON: 161279. 5596gt 3401nt 10066dwt. 426.0 x 58.0 x 26.0ft. (440.2ft
loa). Shelter deck.

*ANGLO-CANADIAN (2).*

Q.4-cyl. engine by North Eastern Marine Engineering Co Ltd, Newcastle. Cylinders $23\frac{1}{2}''/32\frac{1}{2}''/47''/68''$ x 48'' stroke. 3 boilers, 220lb pressure. 2000ihp. Speed $10\frac{1}{4}$knots. 21.1.1929: laid down. 5.7.1929: launched by Short Bros Ltd, Sunderland (Yard No: 437). 14.8.1929: completed for Nitrate Producers' S.S. Co Ltd (Lawther, Latta & Co Ltd, managers), London. 21.8.1940: sunk by gunfire and torpedo from the German auxiliary cruiser WIDDER in 26°10'N 34°09'W while on a voyage from Newport for Bahia Blanca with a cargo of coal.

*ANGLO-AFRICAN (2) with Sydney Harbour Bridge in background.*
*(I.J. Farquhar Collection)*

### 28.   ANGLO-AFRICAN (2)   (1929-1943)
ON: 161339. 5601gt 3369nt 10066dwt. 426.0 x 58.0 x 26.0ft. (439.7ft loa). Shelter deck.
Q.4-cyl. engine by North Eastern Marine Engineering Co Ltd, Newcastle. Cylinders $23\frac{1}{2}''/32\frac{1}{2}''/47''/68''$ x 48'' stroke. 3 boilers, 220lb pressure. 2000ihp. Speed $10\frac{1}{4}$knots.
4.6.1929: laid down. 28.10.1929: launched by Short Bros Ltd, Sunderland (Yard No: 439). 13.12.1929: completed for Nitrate Producers' S.S. Co Ltd (Lawther, Latta & Co Ltd. managers), London. 1943: sold to Reardon Smith Line Ltd (Sir William Reardon Smith & Sons Ltd, managers), Cardiff. 1948: renamed NEW WESTMINSTER CITY. 1949: sold to Sojozita Sg Co Ltd (M.E.

Lentakis, manager), London, renamed LORD CODRINGTON. 1949: sold to Normanton S.S. Co Ltd (Ships Finance & Management Co Ltd, managers), London. 1952: sold to Tozai Kisen K.K., Yokohama, Japan, renamed TOZAI MARU No 7. 1956: sold to Kusakabe Kisen K.K. (Mitsui-O.S.K. Lines K.K., managers), Kobe, Japan, renamed RISSHUN MARU No 3. 1965: broken up in Japan.

### 29.  ANGLO-INDIAN (2)  (1938-1943)

ON: 166338. 5609gt 3341nt 9850dwt. 433.1 x 61.5 x 26.1ft. (447.4ft loa). Shelter deck. Arcform hull.
Reheater T.3-cyl. engine by North Eastern Marine Engineering Co Ltd, Newcastle. Cylinders 24''/39''/68'' x 48'' stroke. 2 boilers, 220lb pressure. 2000ihp. Speed 11 knots.
30.4.1937: laid down. 18.11.1937: launched by Short Bros Ltd, Sunderland (Yard No: 453). 21.1.1938: completed for Nitrate Producers' S.S. Co Ltd (Lawther, Latta & Co Ltd, managers), London. 1943: sold to Reardon Smith Line Ltd (Sir William Reardon Smith & Sons Ltd, managers), Cardiff. 1948: renamed TACOMA CITY. 1954: sold to Williamson & Co Ltd, Hong Kong, renamed INCHCASTLE. 1966: sold to Wing On S.S. Co S.A. (Winley Sg Co, managers), Hong Kong, renamed LUCKY (Panamanian flag). 8.11.1969: arrived at Kaohsiung for breaking up.

*ANGLO-INDIAN (2) at Cape Town in the colours of Sir William Reardon Smith & Sons. Note she is still fitted with life rafts.*                    *(A. Duncan)*

# Southern Steam Shipping Company Ltd

## S1. SOUTH AFRICA (1897-1900)

ON: 108261. 3424gt 2213nt 5800dwt. 352.3 x 45.0 x 17.2/25.1ft. Spar deck.
T.3-cyl. engine by W. Allan & Co Ltd, Sunderland. Cylinders 25''/40''/67'' x 45'' stroke. 2 boilers, 180lb pressure. 1660ihp. Speed 10 knots.
24.4.1897: laid down. 14.9.1897: launched by Short Bros, Sunderland (Yard No: 268). 13.11.1897: completed for Southern Steam Shipping Co Ltd (Lawther, Latta & Co, managers), London. 1900: sold to Cia Marit Union (F.M. Rodas, manager), Bilbao, Spain, renamed NEPTUNO. 25.11.1902: foundered in the Bay of Biscay while on a voyage from Antwerp for Tampico with a cargo of rails and coke.

*RIO BLANCO, ex SOUTH AUSTRALIA.*        *(I.W. Rooke Collection)*

## S2. SOUTH AUSTRALIA (1899-1913)

ON: 110177. 4014gt 2580nt 7050dwt. 370.3 x 48.1 x 20.3/28.9ft. Spar deck.
T.3-cyl. engine by Blair & Co Ltd, Stockton. Cylinders 26''/42''/70'' x 48'' stroke. 3 boilers, 180lb pressure. 2000ihp. Speed 12 knots.
26.11.1898: laid down. 10.7.1899: launched by Short Bros, Sunderland (Yard No: 284). 16.9.1899: completed for Southern Steam Shipping Co Ltd (Lawther, Latta & Co, managers), London. 1907: transferred to Nitrate Producers' S.S. Co Ltd (Lawther, Latta & Co, managers), London. 1913: sold to Petersen & Co Ltd, London, renamed RIO BLANCO. 1914: transferred to London-American Maritime Trading Co Ltd (Petersen & Co Ltd, managers), London. 1918: transferred to Thompson Steam Shipping Co Ltd (Petersen & Co Ltd, managers), London. 1920: sold to Domingo Mumbro S.A., Barcelona, Spain, renamed PEPITO MUMBRO. 16.9.1921: wrecked at Grimorarne, 8 miles south of Uto while of a voyage from Petrograd for the Tyne in ballast.

## S3. SOUTH AMERICA (1900-1912)

ON: 112738. 4197gt 2701nt 7700dwt. 370.3 x 48.7 x 18.9/27.4ft. Spar deck.
T.3-cyl. engine by Blair & Co Ltd, Stockton. Cylinders 26''/42''/70'' x 48'' stroke. 3 boilers, 180lb pressure. 2000ihp. Speed 11 knots.

16.9.1899: laid down. 1.6.1900: launched by Short Bros, Sunderland (Yard No: 291). 14.8.1900: completed for Southern Steam Shipping Co Ltd (Lawther, Latta & Co, managers), London. 1907: transferred to Nitrate Producers' S.S. Co Ltd (Lawther, Latta & Co, managers), London. 13.3.1912: wrecked at St Loy, 6 miles west of Penzance while on a voyage from Hamburg for Cardiff in ballast.

SOUTH AMERICA, a wreck                                              (Gibson & Sons)

## S4. ANGLO-BOLIVIAN (1906-1916)
ON: 123758. 5503gt 3520nt 9300dwt. 418.2 x 54.4 x 29.3ft. Shelter deck. Q.4-cyl. engine by North Eastern Marine Engineering Co Ltd, Newcastle. Cylinders $24\frac{1}{2}''/35''/51''/74''$ x 51'' stroke. 3 boilers, 200lb pressure. 3000ihp. Speed 11 knots.
7.2.1906: laid down. 3.10.1906: launched by Short Bros Ltd, Sunderland (Yard No: 335). 5.12.1906: completed for Southern Steam Shipping Co Ltd (Lawther, Latta & Co, managers), London. 1907: transferred to Nitrate Producers' S.S. Co Ltd (Lawther, Latta & Co, managers), London. 1916: sold to Cunard S.S. Co Ltd, Liverpool, renamed VINOVIA. 19.12.1917: torpedoed and sunk by U105, 8 miles south of Wolf Rock while on a voyage from New York for London with general cargo.

ANGLO-BOLIVIAN.

94

# Seafield Shipping Company Ltd

### S11. BLANEFIELD (1898-1906)
ON: 108382. 3411gt 2182nt 5800dwt. 352.2 x 45.1 x 17.2/25.1ft. Spar deck.
T.3-cyl. engine by G. Clark Ltd, Sunderland. Cylinders $24\frac{1}{2}''/40''/66''$ x 45''
stroke. 2 boilers, 180lb pressure. 1600ihp. Speed 10 knots.
6.11.1897: laid down. 3.6.1898: launched by Short Bros, Sunderland (Yard
No: 270). 6.8.1898: completed for Seafield Shipping Co Ltd (Lawther, Latta
& Co, managers), London. 1.5.1906: sunk following collision with the
4-masted barque KATE THOMAS off Beachy Head while on a voyage from
Junin for Dover (for orders) with a cargo of nitrate of soda.

### S12. WINKFIELD (1900-1912)
ON: 112669. 4009gt 2575nt 7050dwt. 370.4 x 48.1 x 20.3/28.8ft. Spar
deck.
T.3-cyl. engine by G. Clark Ltd, Sunderland. Cylinders 26''/43''/71'' x 51''
stroke. 2 boilers, 180lb pressure. 2250ihp. Speed 12 knots.
3.6.1899: laid down. 19.12.1899: launched by Short Bros, Sunderland (Yard
No: 287). 17.2.1900: completed for Seafield Shipping Co Ltd (Lawther, Latta
& Co, managers), London. 1907: transferred to Nitrate Producers' S.S. Co
Ltd (Lawther, Latta & Co, managers), London. 1912: sold to Russian S.N. &
Trading Co, Odessa, Russia, renamed SADKO. 18.2.1926: breaking up
commenced by T.W. Ward Ltd, Grays, Essex.

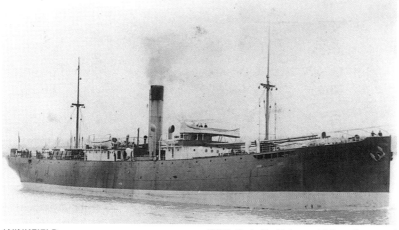

*WINKFIELD.*          *(Bibliothek für Zeitgeschichte, Stuttgart)*

95

## S13. ANGLO-SAXON (1) (1902-1926)

ON: 115813. 4263gt 2671nt 7250dwt. 380.3 x 50.2 x 19.3/27.9ft. Spar deck.
T.3-cyl. engine by G. Clark Ltd, Sunderland. Cylinders 28''/45''/76'' x 51'' stroke. 2 boilers, 180lb pressure. 2625ihp. Speed 12 knots.
13.7.1901: laid down. 24.2.1902: launched by Short Bros, Sunderland (Yard No: 304). 31.5.1902: completed for Seafield Shipping Co Ltd (Lawther, Latta & Co, managers), London. 1907: transferred to Nitrate Producers' S.S. Co Ltd (Lawther, Latta & Co, managers), London. 1926: sold to S.A. Industria Armamento (Pietro Ravano fu Marco, manager), Genoa, Italy, renamed HUMANITAS. 8.4.1930: arrived at Rotterdam in tow, having lost propeller, sold and broken up by Frank Rijsdijk's Industrieele Ondernemingen N.V., Hendrik-Ido-Ambacht.

*ANGLO-COLOMBIAN (1)*                          *(World Ship Photo Library)*

## S14. ANGLO-COLOMBIAN (1) (1907-1915)

ON: 125602. 4792gt 3006nt 8150dwt. 394.8 x 52.5 x 27.9ft. Shelter deck.
Q.4-cyl. engine by North Eastern Marine Engineering Co Ltd, Newcastle. Cylinders 24''/34''/49''/71'' x 48'' stroke. 3 boilers, 220lb pressure. 2700ihp. Speed 11 knots.
28.11.1906: laid down. 29.5.1907: launched by Short Bros Ltd, Sunderland (Yard No: 339). 21.8.1907: completed for Seafield Shipping Co Ltd (Lawther, Latta & Co, managers), London. 1907: transferred to Nitrate Producers' S.S. Co Ltd (Lawther, Latta & Co, managers), London. 23.9.1915: sunk by gunfire from U41, 79 miles southeast of Fastnet while on a voyage from Quebec for Avonmouth with a cargo of horses.

# Managed Ships

## M1. HUNSGATE (1914-1915)
ON: 136815. 3220gt 1978nt. 365.9 x 49.8 x 20.4ft.
T.3-cyl. engine by builders. Cylinders 600/970/1575mm x 1050mm stroke.
2 boilers, 192lb pressure. 1500ihp. Speed 9½ knots.
3.11.1911: launched by Bremer Vulkan, Vegesack (Yard No: 550). 12.1911:
completed for D.G. Argo, Bremen, Germany, as ALTAIR. 11.8.1914: captured
by HMS DUKE OF EDINBURGH in the Red Sea. 1914: The Admiralty (Lawther,
Latta & Co, managers), London, renamed HUNSGATE. 1915: management
transferred to W. Robertson, Glasgow. 1920: sold to A/S Det Selmerske
Rederi, Trondheim, Norway, renamed GURTH. 1924: sold to Les Cargoes
Algeriens S.A., Algiers, Algeria, renamed MOGHREB ACSA. 14.7.1928:
wrecked near Honfleur while on a voyage from Algiers for Rouen with a cargo
of wine.

WAR WAGTAIL as Cunard's VINDELIA  (World Ship Photo Library)

## M2. WAR WAGTAIL (1918-1919)
ON: 142653. 4430gt 2698nt 7020dwt. 376.0 x 51.9 x 26.4ft. Two deck.
T.3-cyl. engine by Central Marine Engine Works Ltd, Hartlepool. Cylinders
27"/44"/73" x 48" stroke. 3 boilers, 180lb pressure. 2644ihp. Speed 11.3
knots.
25.7.1918: launched by W. Gray & Co Ltd, West Hartlepool (Yard No: 906).
9.1918: completed for The Shipping Controller (Lawther, Latta & Co,
managers), London. 1919: sold to Cunard S.S. Co Ltd, Liverpool, renamed
VINDELIA. 1919: transferred to Anchor Line (Henderson Bros) Ltd, Glasgow.
1924: sold to Scindia S.N. Co Ltd, Bombay, India, renamed JALAJYOTI. 1949:
sold for breaking up, commenced 3.1950 by Hindustan Iron Co, Bombay.

**M3. (War Redtail)**
ON: 143404. 4514gt 2732nt 7020dwt. 376.0 x 51.9 x 26.5ft. Two deck. T.3-cyl. engine by Central Marine Engine Works, Hartlepool. Cylinders 27"/44"/73" x 48" stroke. 3 boilers, 180lb pressure. 2644ihp. Speed 11.3 knots.
27.6.1919: launched by W. Gray & Co Ltd, West Hartlepool (Yard No: 913) as WAR REDTAIL for The Shipping Controller (to be managed by Lawther, Latta & Co), London. Sold and 9.1919: completed as HOMAYUN for Bombay & Persia S.N. Co Ltd, Bombay, India. 1929: sold to G. Trilivas & A.G. Vlassopoulos (J.M. Caravas, manager), Piraeus, Greece, renamed AGHIOS MARKOS. 22.4.1941: bombed by German aircraft and sunk off Salamis Island while on a voyage from Buenos Aires for Piraeus.

BERMUDA                                        (World Ship Photo Library)

**M4. BERMUDA (1919-1921)**
ON: 110562. 7027gt 4463nt. 469.4 x 56.2 x 31.9ft. Shelter deck. T.3-cyl engine by Wallsend Slipway Co Ltd, Newcastle. Cylinders 22"/37"/61" x 48" stroke. 3 boilers, 180lb pressure. 3600ihp. Speed 11½ knots.
29.12.1898: launched by C.S. Swan & Hunter Ltd, Newcastle (Yard No: 242). 3.1899: completed as SAINT ANDREW for British & Foreign S.S. Co Ltd (Rankin, Gilmour & Co Ltd, managers), Liverpool. 1911: sold to Hamburg-Amerika Linie, Hamburg, Germany, renamed BERMUDA. 29.3.1919: arrived Firth of Forth, surrendered to Allied Shipping Commission, allocated to Britain, The Shipping Controller (Lawther, Latta & Co, managers), London. 1921: sold to Hajee Nemazee, Bombay, India, renamed ENGLESTAN. 1924: sold to Oriental Nav Co Ltd, Hong Kong. 1925: sold to L. & G.B. Mortola & E. Bozzo (F. & R. Bozzo, managers), Genoa, Italy, renamed MARIA ADELE. 14.9.1932: arrived at Savona for breaking up.

**M5. ERFURT (1919-1920)**
ON: 143131. 7853gt 4896nt. 476.2 x 60.7 x 32.9ft. Two deck. T.3-cyl. engine by builders. Cylinders 820/1340/2200mm x 1400mm stroke. 4 boilers, 200lb pressure. 4000ihp. Speed 13 knots.
6.11.1915: launched by Bremer Vulkan Sch & Masch, Vegesack (Yard No: 583). 4.1919: completed for Norddeutscher Lloyd, Bremen, Germany. 5.4.1919: arrived U.K. port, surrendered to Allied Shipping Commission, allocated to Britain, The Shipping Controller (Lawther, Latta & Co, managers), London. 1920: re-allocated to Belgium. 1922: sold to Lloyd Royal Belge S.A., Antwerp,

*ERFURT as the Belgian flag MERCIER*          *(World Ship Photo Library)*

Belgium, renamed MERCIER. 1930: owners restyled, following merger, Cie Maritime Belge (Lloyd Royal) S.A., Antwerp, Belgium. 9.6.1941: torpedoed and sunk by U204 in 48°30'N 41°30'W, NE of St John's, Newfoundland, while on a voyage from Liverpool for Montreal with a cargo of mail, aircraft and ballast.

### M6. FÜRST BÜLOW (1919-1921)
ON: 143080. 7638gt 4799nt. 469.8 x 58.2 x 32.4ft. Two deck. Two C.2-cyl. engines by builders. Cylinders 650/1585mm x 1370mm stroke. 4 boilers, 205lb pressure. 3400ihp. Speed 11½ knots. Twin screw.
17.12.1910: launched by Bremer Vulkan Sch & Masch, Vegesack (Yard No: 539). 6.1911: completed for Hamburg-Amerika Linie, Hamburg, Germany. 6.11.1915 to 3.2.1917: commissioned as mother ship for minesweeping boats, III Minenraum Div. 30.3.1919: arrived Firth of Forth, surrendered to Allied Shipping Commission, allocated to Britain, The Shipping Controller (Lawther, Latta & Co, managers), London. 1921: sold to Hamburg-Amerika Linie, Hamburg, Germany. 9.1.1933: sold to Blohm & Voss, Hamburg and 5.1934: breaking up commenced.

### M7. ASTORIA (1940?)
4454gt 2094nt 8370dwt. 379.6 x 58.3 x 25.3ft. Shelter deck. Two 6-cyl. 4-stroke, single-acting diesel engines by Burmeister & Wain, Copenhagen. Cylinders 550mm x 1000mm stroke. 2300bhp. Speed 11 knots. Twin screw.
19.1.1926: launched by A/S Nakskov Skibsvaerft, Nakskov (Yard No: 26). 4.1926: completed for D/S Orient A/S, Copenhagen, Denmark. 1940: Minister of Shipping (Lawther, Latta & Co Ltd, managers), London. 1940: Commonwealth Government, Canberra, Australia. 1945: returned to Danish owners. 1954: sold to Oliscal Cia Nav Ltda, San Jose, Costa Rica (A. & G. Frangistas, Lisbon, Portugal, managers), renamed PANAGHIA. 15.2.1960: arrived at La Spezia for breaking up.

**M8.  EMPIRE SUNRISE  (1941-1942)**
ON: 168665. 7459gt 4516nt. 426.0 x 59.9 x 35.0ft. Two deck.
T.3-cyl. engine by G. Clark (1938) Ltd, Sunderland. Cylinders 24''/39''/68''
x 48'' stroke. 2 boilers, 220lb pressure. 2000ihp. Speed 10½ knots.
13.11.1940: launched by J.L. Thompson & Sons Ltd, Sunderland (Yard No:
604). 3.1941: completed for Ministry of War Transport (Lawther, Latta & Co
Ltd, managers), London. 2.11.1942: torpedoed by U402 and abandoned in
51°50'N 46°25'W while on a voyage from Three Rivers for Belfast with a
cargo of steel and timber. Derelict later torpedoed and sunk by U84.

*Erik Hansen with a photograph of his father Oscar Hansen, carpenter on ANGLO-
SAXON (2) when sunk in 1940.*

# Appendix 1

# Company data

Lawther, Latta and Company Ltd
Company No: 178262. Incorporated: 7 December 1921. Voluntary liquidation: 1942.
Capital: £100,000.
Directors:
    Sir John Latta, Bt
    William Latta
    Sir Andrew Gibson Latta, KBE


Nitrate Producers' Steamship Company Ltd
Company No: 43458. Incorporated: 4 March 1895. Voluntary liquidation: 17 September 1918.
Capital: £100,000 (£5 shares). December 1907 increased to £400,000 (half 5% cumulative preference shares).
Directors (1895-1918 unless otherwise stated):

| | | |
|---|---|---|
| George Fleming (chairman 1895-1899) | | died 20.6.1899 |
| John Young Short | | died 4.1.1900 |
| Sir Theodore Fry, Bt | | died 5.2.1912 |
| Gamble North | | |
| John Latta (chairman 1899-1918) | appointed 1899 | |
| Thomas Smart Short | appointed 1900 | |
| Gilbert Gordon Blane | appointed 1908 | |
| Vice-Admiral Orford Churchill | appointed 1908 | died 1.12.1909 |


Southern Steam Shipping Company Ltd
Company No: 49679. Incorporated: 10 October 1896. Voluntary liquidation: 26 November 1907.
Capital: £100,000 (£10 shares).
Directors (1896-1907)
    John Latta
    Robert Allen Lawther
    Thomas Smart Short
    Ernest Withers Short
    John Young Short, Jr
    Joseph Short


Seafield Shipping Company Ltd
Company No: 50568. Incorporated: 17.12.1896. Voluntary liquidation: 31.1.1908.
Capital: £35,000 (£5 shares). November 1899 increased to £100,000.
Directors (1896-1908):

| | |
|---|---|
| Gilbert Gordon Blane (chairman) | |
| Samuel Lawther | |
| Robert Allen Lawther | |
| Vice-Admiral Sir George T.H. Boyes, KCB | resigned 1900 |
| Vice-Admiral Orford Churchill | appointed 1900 |


Nitrate Producers' Steamship Company Ltd
Company No: 151602. Incorporated: 5 October 1918. Voluntary liquidation: 27 November 1942.
Capital: £200,000 (£5 shares). £156,300 issued.
Directors (1918-1942 unless otherwise stated):

| | |
|---|---|
| John Latta (chairman 1918-1942) (1920: Sir John Latta, Bt) | |
| Gamble North | died 21.7.1921 |
| Robert Allen Lawther | died 22.3.1941 |
| Thomas Smart Short, JP | |

Gilbert Gordon Blane, JP                                    died 24.11.1928
Cecil Latta                    appointed 1928              died 26.12.1937
Sir Andrew Gibson Latta, KBE   appointed 1937
Albert Edward Holdsworth       appointed 1941

# Flags and funnels

As has been mentioned the houseflag and funnel markings of the Nitrate Producers' Steamship Company were taken from Colonel North's racing colours, light blue with primrose sleeves, primrose five pointed stars and a scarlet cap. There is also an affinity with the national colours of Chile, the Chilean flag carrying a white five pointed star on a blue ground with the flag divided horizontally into blue and white over red.

Both the Nitrate Producers' Steamship Companies employed a black funnel with two bands, blue over red. Centred on these bands was a yellow five pointed star. The flag had, on a red ground, a blue diamond with a similar yellow star, with in each corner of the red ground the black letters N P S C.

The Seafield Shipping Company and Southern Steam Shipping Company both adopted yellow funnels with black tops, the only difference being Southern placed a black S on the yellow. Both flew flags with a blue St George's Cross on a white ground. Again the Southern company differentiated by adding a red square in the centre carrying a black S.

All these three flags were square which was rather unusual, as few chose to adopt such proportions. They were also numbered amongst the small band who flew a managers' burgee with the houseflag.

Lawther, Latta and Company flew a different burgee with each of the companies. That for Nitrate Producers' Steamship Company was a blue ground edged red top and bottom, the Seafield Shipping Company burgee was blue and the Southern Steam Shipping Company was blue and white with blue to the hoist. All three carried the letters LL close to the hoist.

# Return on investment

Return on investment of £100 in Nitrate Producers' Steamship Company Ltd in 1895—twenty £5 shares:

| | |
|---|---:|
| Interest paid 1896-1918 264.25% | £  264.25 |
| On winding up £35 War Loans plus £5 share in new company per share. War Loan, face value | 700.00 |
| Interest paid 1919-1942 247.5% | 247.50 |
| Distribution of assets on winding up £28 at once, £7 to follow per share | 700.00 |
| | £1,911.75 |

Note.- The market price of War Loan stock when offered in October 1918 was approximately £95%.

Nitrate Producers' Steamship Company Ltd.

Seafield Shipping Company Ltd.

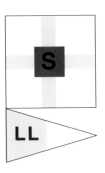

Southern Steam Shipping Company Ltd.

# Appendix 4

## The Nitrate Producers' Steamship Company Limited

(all figures £,000)

| Year ended 30 April | Issued Capital £ | 5% cum. Pref Shares £ | Reserve Accounts £ | 5% Treasury Guarantee Loan £ | Creditors & Bills payable £ | Fleet Value £ | Investments £ | Paid on account of new tonnage £ | Cash and Debtors £ | Profit & Loss Account £ | To Depreciation & Reserves £ | Dividend % |
|---|---|---|---|---|---|---|---|---|---|---|---|---|
| 1896 | 63 | — | — | — | 1 | 59 | — | — | 8 | 5 | 2 | 7½ |
| 1897 | 85 | — | — | — | 1 | 93 | — | — | 7 | 12 | 7 | 7½ |
| 1898 | 91 | — | — | — | 3 | 87 | — | 5 | 6 | 21 | 11 | 7½ |
| 1899 | 100 | — | 1 | — | 6 | 104 | — | — | 7 | 32 | 23 | 7½ |
| 1900 | 100 | — | 1 | — | 7 | 97 | — | — | 18 | 39 | 25 | 10 |
| 1901 | 100 | — | 1 | — | 22 | 111 | — | — | 20 | 60 | 45 | 10 |
| 1902 | 100 | — | 2 | — | 54 | 150 | — | — | 13 | 48 | 32 | 10 |
| 1903 | 100 | 94 | 3 | — | 40 | 133 | — | — | 15 | 35 | 17 | 10 |
| 1904 | 100 | 110 | 3 | — | 31 | 122 | — | — | 18 | 28 | 12 | 7½ |
| 1905 | 100 | 110 | 3 | — | 42 | 110 | — | — | 38 | 27 | 12 | 7½ |
| 1906 | 100 | 110 | 4 | — | 83 | 154 | — | — | 29 | 25 | 10 | 7½ |
| 1907 | 100 | 110 | 1 | — | 8 | 83 | — | — | 30 | 25 | 12 | 7½ |
| 1908 | 156 | 110 | 2 | — | 186 | 369 | 30 | 68 | 76 | 33 | 9 | 7½ |
| 1909 | 156 | 110 | 1 | — | 127 | 326 | 49 | — | 75 | 45 | 23 | 7½ |
| 1910 | 156 | 110 | 2 | — | 91 | 305 | 82 | 50 | 61 | 50 | 22 | 6¼ |
| 1911 | 156 | 110 | 3 | — | 122 | 331 | 312 | — | 68 | 65 | 35 | 7½ |
| 1912 | 156 | 110 | 14 | — | 49 | 229 | 725 | — | 44 | 80 | 68 | 8 |
| 1913 | 156 | 110 | 60 | — | 32 | 252 | 547 | — | 90 | 133 | 144 | 12½ |
| 1914 | 156 | 110 | 92 | — | 49 | 266 | — | — | 107 | 136 | 100 | 12½ |
| 1915 | 156 | 110 | 102 | — | 88 | 167 | — | — | 182 | 152 | 100 | 17½ |
| 1916 | 156 | 110 | 994* | — | 98 | 785 | — | — | 403 | 404 | 130 | 25 |
| 1917 | 156 | 110 | 1120* | — | 166 | 804 | — | — | 67 | 426 | 138 | 30 |
| 1918 | 156 | 110 | 1378* | — | 167 | 1094 | — | — | 208 | 240 | 90 | 30 |

NOTES:

RESERVE ACCOUNTS — The total of all accounts such as Insurance Fund, General reserve Fund, Deferred Building Fund, Capital Reserve Account, Special Emergency Reserve Account and Tax Reserves.
Between 1920 and 1929 fleet value and investment was given as a single combined figure.

*including £200,000 reserve for excess profits tax and £662,000 building fund
*including £220,000 reserve for excess profits tax and £700,000 building fund
*including £100,000 reserve for excess profits tax and £700,000 building fund

| Year | | | | | | | | | | | | | |
|------|---|---|---|---|---|---|---|---|---|---|---|---|---|
| 1919* | 156 | — | 573* | — | — | 93 | 219 | 555 | — | 54 | 66 | — | 15 |
| 1920 | 156 | — | 636* | — | — | 204 | 940 | — | — | 83 | 160 | 75 | 15 |
| 1921 | 156 | — | 743 | — | — | 104 | 952 | — | — | 67 | 92* | 90 | 15 |
| 1922 | 156 | — | 685 | — | — | 77 | 832 | — | — | 131 | 108* | 50 | 15 |
| 1923 | 156 | — | 567 | — | — | 44 | 757 | — | — | 52 | 48* | 25 | 10 |
| 1924 | 156 | — | 571 | — | — | 48 | 752 | — | — | 50 | 40 | — | 10 |
| 1925 | 156 | — | 560 | — | — | 42 | 738 | — | — | 46 | 55 | 15 | 10 |
| 1926 | 156 | — | 552 | — | — | 17 | 709 | — | — | 41 | 51 | 25 | 10 |
| 1927 | 156 | — | 553 | — | — | 10 | 712 | — | — | 33 | 93 | 70 | 10 |
| 1928 | 156 | — | 554 | — | 180 | 33 | 781 | — | 75 | 92 | 107 | 70 | 10 |
| 1929 | 156 | — | 555 | — | 150 | 17 | 751 | — | 120 | 32 | 91 | 55 | 10 |
| 1930 | 156 | — | 551 | — | 120 | 54 | 432 | 417 | — | 57 | 96 | 60 | 10 |
| 1931 | 156 | — | 538 | — | 90 | 30 | 372 | 408 | — | 55 | 54 | 24 | 7½ |
| 1932 | 156 | — | 511 | — | 60 | 19 | 343 | 383 | — | 44 | 43 | 30* | 7½ |
| 1933 | 156 | — | 497 | — | 30 | 19 | 318 | 373 | — | 35 | 39 | 40* | 7½ |
| 1934 | 156 | — | 475 | — | — | 33 | 290 | 363 | — | 35 | 29 | 38* | 7½ |
| 1935 | 156 | — | 471 | — | — | 24 | 281 | 363 | — | 30 | 28 | 13 | 6¼ |
| 1936 | 156 | — | 483 | — | — | 6 | 251 | 363 | — | 54 | 65* | 48 | 6¼ |
| 1937 | 156 | — | 500 | — | — | 17 | 154 | 463 | 22 | 68 | 73* | 43 | 7½ |
| 1938 | 156 | — | 529 | — | — | 23 | 189 | 463 | — | 94 | 145 | 114 | 12½ |
| 1939 | 156 | — | 557 | — | — | 15 | 101 | 615 | — | 48 | 66 | 38 | 10 |
| 1940 | 156 | — | 565 | — | — | 34 | 101 | 615 | — | 75 | 67 | 13 | 10 |
| 1941 | 156 | — | 739 | — | — | 54 | 63 | 594 | — | 342 | 74 | — | 10 |
| 1942 | 156 | — | 738 | — | — | 58 | 46 | 479 | — | 478 | 48 | — | 15 |

*including £65,000 reserve for excess profits tax.  *6 months only.
*includes £130,000 reserve for excess profits tax.

*after excess profits duty of £332,271.
*including £147,906 from Emergency Reserve.
*including £66,037 from Emergency Reserve.

*including £17,000 from Insurance Fund.
*including £18,000 from Insurance Fund.
*including £20,000 from Insurance Fund.

*including £17,773 Tramp Shipping Freight Subsidy.
*including £20,679 Tramp Shipping Freight Subsidy.

# Appendix 5

# Prices paid and obtained for ships

The prices paid are believed to have been the contract prices, the final sums paid were invariably higher to cover changes ordered during construction. The amounts realised are as reported in the press and were probably subject to adjustment.

| Name | Blt/Bt | GT | Paid | Sold | Realised |
|------|--------|------|--------|--------|----------|
| COLONEL J T NORTH | 95 | 2835 | £ 27,350 | 1897 | not known |
| AVERY HILL | 95 | 3142 | 31,000 | 1899 | not known |
| JUANITA NORTH | 96 | 3503 | 33,650 | 1906 | £ 21,500 |
| GEORGE FLEMING | 97 | 3448 | 36,000 | 1911 | 17,000 |
| SOUTH AFRICA | 97 | 3424 | 34,000 | 1900 | 43,500 |
| BLANEFIELD | 98 | 3411 | 35,000 | 1906* | not known |
| ANGLO-CHILIAN | 98 | 3817 | 39,250 | 1911 | 23,000 |
| ANGLO-AUSTRALIAN (1) | 99 | 4019 | 47,650 | 1915 | 68,750 |
| SOUTH AUSTRALIA | 99 | 4014 | 48,000 | 1913 | 35,500 |
| WINKFIELD | 00 | 4009 | 54,000 | 1912 | 35,000 |
| SOUTH AMERICA | 00 | 4197 | 54,500 | 1912* | 31,000 |
| ANGLO-AFRICAN (1) | 00 | 4186 | 55,500 | 1909* | 36,000 |
| ANGLO-CANADIAN (1) | 01 | 4239 | 66,750 | 1918** | not known |
| ANGLO-SAXON (1) | 02 | 4263 | 61,900 | 1926 | 11,500 |
| ANGLO-PERUVIAN (1) | 05 | 5494 | 64,300 | 1906* | not known |
| ANGLO-BOLIVIAN | 06 | 5503 | 70,000 | 1916 | 190,000 |
| ANGLO-COLOMBIAN (1) | 07 | 4792 | 63,800 | 1915** | 60,000 |
| ANGLO-MEXICAN | 08 | 4796 | 64,500 | 1927 | 28,000 |
| ANGLO-PATAGONIAN | 10 | 5017 | 57,500 | 1917** | 73,900 |
| ANGLO-CALIFORNIAN | 12 | 7333 | 69,575 | 1915 | 215,000 |
| ANGLO-EGYPTIAN | 12 | 7379 | 73,050 | 1927 | 41,500 |
| ANGLO-BRAZILIAN | 13 | 7486 | 87,700 | 1915 | 200,000 |
| ANGLO-CHILEAN | 16 | 9097 | 102,000 | 1930 | 40,000 |
| ANGLO-COLOMBIAN (2) | 15/21 | 8407 | 60,000 | 1936 | 25,000 |
| ANGLO-INDIAN (1) | 25 | 5531 | 100,000 | 1937 | 50,000 |
| ANGLO-PERUVIAN (2) | 26 | 5457 | 91,500 | 1941** | 125,000 |
| ANGLO-AUSTRALIAN (2) | 27 | 5456 | 91,500 | 1938* | not known |
| ANGLO-CANADIAN (2) | 28 | 5268 | 130,000 | 1942** | 152,243 |
| ANGLO-SAXON (2) | 29 | 5596 | 95,000 | 1940** | 125,000 |
| ANGLO-AFRICAN (2) | 29 | 5601 | 95,000 | 1943 | 125,000 |
| ANGLO-INDIAN (2) | 38 | 5609 | 107,500 | 1943 | 164,000 |
| | | | £2,047,475 | | £1,937,393 |

The 18 ships sold for £1,334,250 cost when new or purchased £1,183,775. That was a profit of £150,475 on sales (12.7%). Adding in ships lost where insured values or claims paid are known, gives us 25 ships for which £1,937,393 was received. They cost when new £1,731,575, giving a profit of £205,818 (11.9%). For marine (*) and war losses (**) insured values are given where known.

# Appendix 6

# Shareholders 11 June 1919
# The Nitrate Producers' Steamship Company Ltd

| Number: | Name, residence, profession: |
|---|---|
| 7,592 | John Latta, London, shipowner |
| 1,821 | John Reeves Ellerman, London, baronet |
| 100 | John Adamson, Sunderland, engineer |
| 216 | Jane Allan, Sunderland, lady |
| 70 | Sir J.S. Barwick, Sunderland ** |
| 260 | Charles Forbes Blane, London, Brigadier General |
| 797 | Gilbert Gordon Blane, Windsor, engineer |
| 26 | Evelyn Pelham Brown, London, married |
| 120 | Emily Byers, Sunderland, married |
| 144 | Cyrille H.D. Bayfield, Hertingfordbury, spinster |
| 600 | British Steamship Investment Trust Ltd, London |
| 200 | Brewery & Commercial Investment Trust Ltd, London |
| 32 | Constance Jessie Boyes, London, spinster |
| 100 | John Bisset and another, Glasgow, esquire |
| 30 | Kathleen Maud Barwick and others, London, spinster |
| 196 | Henry Clark, Sunderland, engineer |
| 150 | William Carter, Sunderland ** |
| 40 | Herbert Alexander Chapman, Blandford, Lieutenant Colonel |
| 307 | Janet Paterson Cameron, Ballycastle, spinster |
| 190 | Janet Cameron and others, Manchester, widow |
| 41 | Eleanor C.R. Churchill, London, spinster |
| 80 | R.C.W. Currie and others, London, esquire |
| 45 | Ashlin Cutforth, London, underwriter |
| 25 | William Holford Dixon, London, esquire |
| 50 | A.E.V. Derrett and another, Budleigh Salterton, esquire |
| 50 | Errington Dawson, Lisbon, merchant |
| 40 | Joseph Fleming, Londonderry ** |
| 50 | Robert Farrow, Sunderland, esquire |
| 805 | Robert H.D. Fleming, London, merchant |
| 236 | Gilbert C. Felce and another, London, esquire |
| 90 | Ethel Mildred Fleming, London, married |
| 137 | Martha Greenwell, Sunderland, widow |
| 38 | Evelyn Ellen Hope, Cardigan, spinster |
| 126 | Douglas Hankey, London, esquire |
| 200 | Susannah Irwing, Sunderland, widow |
| 44 | Annie Morgan Kinsey, Brighton, spinster |
| 44 | Ada K.O. Kinsey, Brighton, spinster |
| 117 | Isabella Kirkpatrick, Ballycastle, married |
| 233 | William Latta, London, esquire |
| 164 | Euphemia Jane Latta, Edinburgh, spinster |
| 173 | Helen Latta, Edinburgh, spinster |
| 246 | Robert Latta, Craigadam, Dalbeattie, near Dumfries, farmer |
| 102 | London Maritime Investment Co Ltd, London |
| 159 | Alice Simpson Latta, Edinburgh, spinster |
| 155 | Alice Latchford, Torquay, spinster |
| 20 | Alexander Wingate Langlands, Glasgow, shipowner |
| 11 | Mary Anne Lott, East Molesley, widow |
| 421 | Andrew Gibson Latta, London, esquire |
| 1,001 | Robert Allen Lawther, London, esquire |
| 414 | London General Investment Trust Ltd, London |
| 2,793 | Ada May Latta, London, married |
| 90 | William Maughan, Hexham ** |
| 30 | Andrew Matthews, London, esquire |
| 20 | Dora Macnair, Edinburgh, married |
| 60 | Benjamin Morton, Sunderland ** |
| 10 | Marie Louise Miles, London, spinster |
| 485 | Mercantile Investment & General Trust Co Ltd, London |
| 75 | James Macalister, London, merchant |
| 259 | Frederick Wolff May, London, esquire |
| 135 | Clara Fanny May, London, spinster |
| 10 | Henry Charles St Lo Malet, London, esquire |

| | |
|---|---|
| 251 | Gamble North, Eridge, merchant |
| 25 | Charles John Obery and another, London, esquire |
| 25 | Rt Hon Baron Pirrie of Belfast, London (KP, PC) |
| 74 | Lilian Annette Paull, Bristol, spinster |
| 33 | Lilian Annette Paull and another, Bristol, spinster |
| 180 | Helen Swann, Lanark, spinster |
| 100 | Charles R.J.A. Swan, London, (MB) |
| 964 | Mary Ada Short, Sunderland, widow |
| 1,156 | Joseph Short, Sunderland ** |
| 643 | Thomas Smart Short, Sunderland, esquire |
| 100 | Samuel Walter Stephens and another, London, esquire |
| 20 | Maggie Simmons, London, married |
| 4,108 | John Y. Short, Sunderland ** |
| 45 | Margaret Latta Smith, Edinburgh, married |
| 45 | Andrew Murdoch Smith, Edinburgh (MA—clerk in holy orders) |
| 48 | James Cockroft Smith, Birkenhead, esquire |
| 400 | George Anderson Short, Sunderland, esquire |
| 100 | Edward John Stannard, London, solicitor |
| 10 | Albert Shreeve, London, chauffeur |
| 68 | Hugh George Sicklemore, Chislehurst, esquire |
| 50 | Jessie Elizabeth Sicklemore, Chislehurst, married |
| 40 | Lady Blanche C. Stewart, London, spinster |
| 150 | Mrs M.F. Todd, Sunderland ** |
| 75 | Mrs J.B. Taylor, Sunderland ** |
| 40 | Jane Beatrice Taylor, Thirsk, married |
| 5 | William Tod and another, Liverpool, esquire |
| 40 | William A. Thompson and another, London, underwriter |
| 30 | John Wigham, Sunderland, esquire |
| 60 | Elizabeth J.S. Walker, Airdrie, married |
| 40 | Charles Wright, London, esquire |
| | ** deceased, in hands of executors. |

ANGLO AFRICAN (2).                    (World Ship Photo Library)

# BIBLIOGRAPHY

Newspapers, magazines and other periodicals:
Belfast News Letter; Belfast Telegraph; Cumnock Chronicle; District Times; Fairplay; Lloyd's Confidential Index; Lloyd's List; Lloyd's Register of Shipping; Manchester Evening News; Marine Engineer & Naval Architect; The Motorship; Sea Breezes; Shipbuilding & Shipping Record; Shipping World; Steamship; Sunderland Echo (Blue Peter's records); Syren & Shipping; The Times.

Books:
Anderson, E.B.—Sailing Ships of Ireland (Impact, Coleraine, 1984)
Ballard, Dr R.D.—The Discovery of the Titanic (Hodder & Stoughton, London, 1987)
Bierman, John—Dark Safari: The life behind the legend of Henry Morton Stanley (Hodder & Stoughton, London, 1991)
Blakemore, H.—British Nitrates & Chilean Politics 1886-1896: Balmaceda & North (Athlone, London, 1974)
Bone, D.W.—Merchantman Rearmed (Chatto & Windus, London, 1949)
Bonwick, G.J.—British Shipping, an Independent Study (Fennbond, Henley)
Brooke, G.—Alarm Starboard (Stephens, London, 1982)
Clifford, H.—The Skagway Story (Alaska Northwest Books, Seattle, 1988)
    —Railways North, the Railroads of Alaska & the Yukon (Superior Publishing, Seattle, 1981)
Crothall, Allan C.—Wealth from the Sea (Starr Line, Orpington, 1993)
Cunynghame, Major Francis de M.—The Long Trail: the Story of the Klondike Gold and the Man Who Fought for Control (Faber & Faber, London, 1953)
Fayle, C.E.—The War and the Shipping Industry (Oxford, 1927)
H.M.S.O.—British Vessels Lost at Sea 1914-1918
    —British Vessels Lost at Sea 1939-1945
Harrison, L.—A Titanic Myth: The Californian Incident (Kimber, London, 1986)
Heaton, P.M.—Reardon Smith Line (Heaton, Cardiff, 1984)
Hernandez C, Roberto—El Salitre (Fisher Hnos, Valparaiso, 1930)
Jones, G.P.—Two Survived (Hamish Hamilton, London, 1941)
Lubbock, B.—The Nitrate Clippers (Brown, Son & Ferguson, Glasgow, 1932)
Martin, Cy—Gold Rush Narrow Gauge (Trans-Anglo Books. Corona del Mar CA, 1974)
Masters, D.—In Peril on the Sea (Cresset, London, 1960)
    —When Ships Go Down (Eyre & Spottiswoode, London, 1932)
Muggenthaler, A.K.—German Raiders of World War II (Hale, London, 1978)
Platt, D.C.M.—Latin America & British Trade (Black, London, 1972)
Ritchie, Carson—Q-Ships (Dalton, Lavenham, 1985)
Rohwer, J. & Hummelchen, G.—Chronology of the War at Sea 1939-1945 (Greenhill, London, 1992)
Rohwer, J.—Axis Submarine Successes 1939-1945 (Stephen, Cambridge, 1983)
Sinclair, Robert C.—Across the Irish Sea (Conway, London, 1990)
Tomlinson, N.—The Most Dangerous Moment (Kimber, London, 1976)
unknown—Mowbray Quay & Pallion Yard 1850-1950 (Short Bros, Sunderland, 1950)
    —La Marina Italiana della Seconda Guerra Mondiale—vol III Navi Mercantili Perdute (Rome, 1977)
Winslow, K.—Big Pan-Out (Travel Book Club, London, 1953)
Winton, J.—The Victoria Cross at Sea (Joseph, London, 1978)

# INDEX OF SHIPS

Names in capitals carried whilst owned/managed by Lawther, Latta and Company and associated companies. Lower case letters are previous or later names. The number is the entry in the fleet list.

Affinita  4
Afrika  22
Aghios Markos  M3
Alcamo  21
Altair  M1
ANGLO-AFRICAN (1)  7
ANGLO-AFRICAN (2)  28
ANGLO-AUSTRALIAN (1)  6
ANGLO-AUSTRALIAN (2)  25
ANGLO-BOLIVIAN  S4
ANGLO-BRAZILIAN  20
ANGLO-CALIFORNIAN  18
ANGLO-CANADIAN (1)  8
ANGLO-CANADIAN (2)  26
ANGLO-CHILEAN  21
ANGLO-CHILIAN  5
ANGLO-COLOMBIAN (1)  S14
ANGLO-COLOMBIAN (2)  22
ANGLO-EGYPTIAN  19
ANGLO-INDIAN (1)  23
ANGLO-INDIAN (2)  29
ANGLO-MEXICAN  16
ANGLO-PATAGONIAN  17
ANGLO-PERUVIAN (1)  9
ANGLO-PERUVIAN (2)  24
ANGLO-SAXON (1)  S13
ANGLO-SAXON (2)  27
Artygia  23
ASTORIA  M7
AVERY HILL  2

Baxtergate  23
BERMUDA  M4
BLANEFIELD  S11
Byzantion  6

Calonne  6
Chepstow Castle  20
COLONEL J.T. NORTH  1

Domina  23
Dunearn  2

Ekaterina C  6
Ekaterina Inglessi  6
Elmsgarth  3
EMPIRE SUNRISE  M8
Englestan  M4
ERFURT  M5

FÜRST BÜLOW  M6

GEORGE FLEMING  4
Gurth  M1 -

Heraclides  21
Hermes  21
Homayun  M3
Humanitas  S13
HUNSGATE  M1

Inchcastle  29
Istok  1

Jalajyoti  M2
JUANITA NORTH  3

Lesteloide  19
Lily Michalos  23
Lord Codrington  28
Lucky  29

Maria Adele  M4
Mercier  M5
Moghreb Acsa  M1
Monreale  16

Neptuno  S1
New Westminster City  28

Olovsborg  19

Panaghia  M7
Pepito Mumbro  S2

Respice Patriam  16
Rio Blanco  S2
Rio Aguassu  5
Risshun Maru No 3  28

Sadko  S12
Saint Andrew  M4
St Francois  21
Schwarzenfels  22
SOUTH AFRICA  S1
SOUTH AMERICA  S3
SOUTH AUSTRALIA  S2

Tacoma City  29
Tozai Maru No 7  28

Vandalia  18
Vindelia  M2
Vinovia  S4

WAR REDTAIL  M3
WAR WAGTAIL  M2
WINKFIELD  S12

ANGLO-SAXON (2) loading logs for Australia in North Vancouver, February 1939.
*(E.E. Milburn)*

Chief Engineer Milburn

Family on board (left). Left to right:
Mrs Laidler, 3rd mate, unidentified,
Mrs Milburn, Chief Engineer Laidler.
ANGLO-COLOMBIAN (2) 1935.
*(E.E. Milburn)*